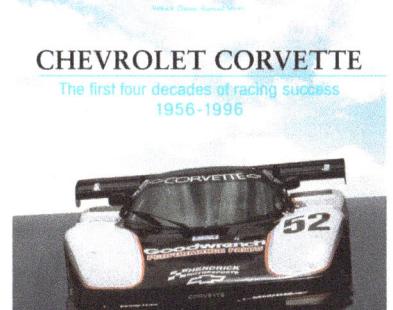

CHEVROLET CORVETTE
The first four decades of racing success
1956-1996

John Starkey

More books from Veloce...

1½-litre GP Racing 1961-1965 (Whitelock)
AC Two-litre Saloons & Buckland Sportscars (Archibald)
Alfa Romeo 155/156/147 Competition Touring Cars (Collins)
Alfa Tipo 33 (McDonough & Collins)
Alpine & Renault – The Development of the Revolutionary Turbo F1 Car 1968 to 1979 (Smith)
Autodrome (Collins & Ireland)
Bahamas Speed Weeks, The (O'Neil)
British at Indianapolis, The (Wagstaff)
British Café Racers (Cloesen)
Bugatti Type 40 (Price)
Bugatti 46/50 Updated Edition (Price & Arbey)
Bugatti T44 & T49 (Price & Arbey)
Bugatti 57 2nd Edition (Price)
Bugatti Type 57 Grand Prix – A Celebration (Tomlinson)
Cosworth – The Search for Power (6th edition) (Robson)
Daily Mirror 1970 World Cup Rally 40, The (Robson)
Datsun Fairlady Roadster to 280ZX – The Z-Car Story (Long)
Fate of the Sleeping Beauties, The (op de Weegh/ Hottendorff/op de Weegh)
Ferrari 288 GTO, The Book of the (Sackey)
Ferrari 333 SP (O'Neil)
Formula One – The Real Score? (Harvey)
Formula 5000 Motor Racing, Back then ... and back now (Lawson)
Forza Minardi! (Vigar)
Grand Prix Ferrari – The Years of Enzo Ferrari's Power, 1948-1980 (Pritchard)
Grand Prix Ford – DFV-powered Formula 1 Cars (Robson)
GT – The World's Best GT Cars 1953-73 (Dawson)
Italian Cafe Racers (Cloesen)
Jaguar E-type Factory and Private Competition Cars (Griffiths)
Lamborghini Miura Bible, The (Sackey)
Lamborghini Murciélago, The book of the (Pathmanathan)
Lamborghini Urraco, The Book of the (Landsem)
Lancia 037 (Collins)
Le Mans Panoramic (Ireland)
Lexus Story, The (Long)
Lola – The Illustrated History (1957-1977) (Starkey)
Lola – All the Sports Racing & Single-seater Racing Cars 1978-1997 (Starkey)
Lola T70 – The Racing History & Individual Chassis Record – 4th Edition (Starkey)
Lotus 18 Colin Chapman's U-turn (Whitelock)
Lotus 49 (Oliver)
Making a Morgan (Hensing)
Maserati 250F In Focus (Pritchard)
Mazda MX-5/Miata 1.6 Enthusiast's Workshop Manual (Grainger & Shoemark)
Mazda MX-5/Miata 1.8 Enthusiast's Workshop Manual (Grainger & Shoemark)
Mazda MX-5 Miata, The book of the – The 'Mk1' NA-series 1988 to 1997 (Long)
Mazda MX-5 Miata, The book of the – The 'Mk2' NB-series 1997 to 2004 (Long)
Mazda MX-5 Miata Roadster (Long)
Mazda Rotary-engined Cars (Cranswick)
Mercedes-Benz SL – R230 series 2001 to 2011 (Long)
Mercedes-Benz SL – W113-series 1963-1971 (Long)
Mercedes-Benz SL & SLC – 107-series 1971-1989 (Long)
Mercedes-Benz SLK – R170 series 1996-2004 (Long)
Mercedes-Benz SLK – R171 series 2004-2011 (Long)
Mercedes-Benz W123-series – All models 1976 to 1986 (Long)
MG, Made in Abingdon (Frampton)
MGB – The Illustrated History, Updated Fourth Edition (Wood & Burrell)
Mike the Bike – Again (Macauley)
Mitsubishi Lancer Evo, The Road Car & WRC Story (Long)
Montlhéry, The Story of the Paris Autodrome (Boddy)
Morris Minor, 70 Years on the Road (Newell)
Moto Guzzi Sport & Le Mans Bible, The (Falloon)
The Moto Guzzi Story – 3rd Edition (Falloon)
Motor Racing – Reflections of a Lost Era (Carter)
Motor Racing – The Pursuit of Victory 1930-1962 (Carter)
Motor Racing – The Pursuit of Victory 1963-1972 (Wyatt/Sears)
Motor Racing Heroes – The Stories of 100 Greats (Newman)
Motorcycle GP Racing in the 1960s (Pereira)
Motorsport In colour, 1950s (Wainwright)
N.A.R.T. – A concise history of the North American Racing Team 1957 to 1983 (O'Neil)
Nissan 300ZX & 350Z – The Z-Car Story (Long)
Nissan GT-R Supercar: Born to race (Gorodji)
Northeast American Sports Car Races 1950-1959 (O'Neil)
Porsche 911R, RS & RSR, 4th Edition (Starkey)
Porsche 930 to 935: The Turbo Porsches (Starkey)
Racing Colours – Motor Racing Compositions 1908-2009 (Newman)
Racing Line – British motorcycle racing in the golden age of the big single (Guntrip)
Rallye Sport Fords: The Inside Story (Moreton)
Rootes Cars of the 50s, 60s & 70s – Hillman, Humber, Singer, Sunbeam & Talbot, A Pictorial History (Rowe)
Rover Cars 1945 to 2005, A Pictorial History
Rover P4 (Bobbitt)
Runways & Racers (O'Neil)
RX-7 – Mazda's Rotary Engine Sportscar (Updated & Revised New Edition) (Long)
Schlumpf – The intrigue behind the most beautiful car collection in the world (Op de Weegh & Op de Weegh)
Sleeping Beauties USA – abandoned classic cars & trucks (Marek)
Speedway – Auto racing's ghost tracks (Collins & Ireland)
Subaru Impreza: The Road Car And WRC Story (Long)
This Day in Automotive History (Corey)
TT Talking – The TT's most exciting era – As seen by Manx Radio TT's lead commentator 2004-2012 (Lambert)
Two Summers – The Mercedes-Benz W196R Racing Car (Ackerson)
TWR Story, The – Group A (Hughes & Scott)
Unraced (Collins)
You & Your Jaguar XK8/XKR – Buying, Enjoying, Maintaining, Modifying – New Edition (Thorley)
Wolseley Cars 1948 to 1975 (Rowe)
Works Rally Mechanic (Moylan)

Veloce's other imprints:

www.veloce.co.uk

First published in 2002 by Gryfon Press. Veloce Classic Reprint (hardback) edition published December 2018. This (paperback) edition published March 2019 by Veloce Publishing Limited, Veloce House, Parkway Farm Business Park, Middle Farm Way, Poundbury, Dorchester DT1 3AR, England. Tel +44 (0)1305 260068 /Fax 01305 250479 / e-mail info@veloce.co.uk / web www.veloce.co.uk or www.velocebooks.com. ISBN: 978-1-787114-92-0 UPC: 6-36847-01492-6

© 2018 & 2019 John Starkey and Veloce Publishing. All rights reserved. With the exception of quoting brief passages for the purpose of review, no part of this publication may be recorded, reproduced or transmitted by any means, including photocopying, without the written permission of Veloce Publishing Ltd. Throughout this book logos, model names and designations, etc, have been used for the purposes of identification, illustration and decoration. Such names are the property of the trademark holder as this is not an official publication. Readers with ideas for automotive books, or books on other transport or related hobby subjects, are invited to write to the editorial director of Veloce Publishing at the above address. British Library Cataloguing in Publication Data – A catalogue record for this book is available from the British Library. Typesetting, design and page make-up all by Veloce Publishing Ltd on Apple Mac.
Printed and bound by CPI Group (UK) Ltd, Croydon, CR0 4YY.

Veloce *Classic Reprint* Series

CHEVROLET CORVETTE

The first four decades of racing success 1956-1996

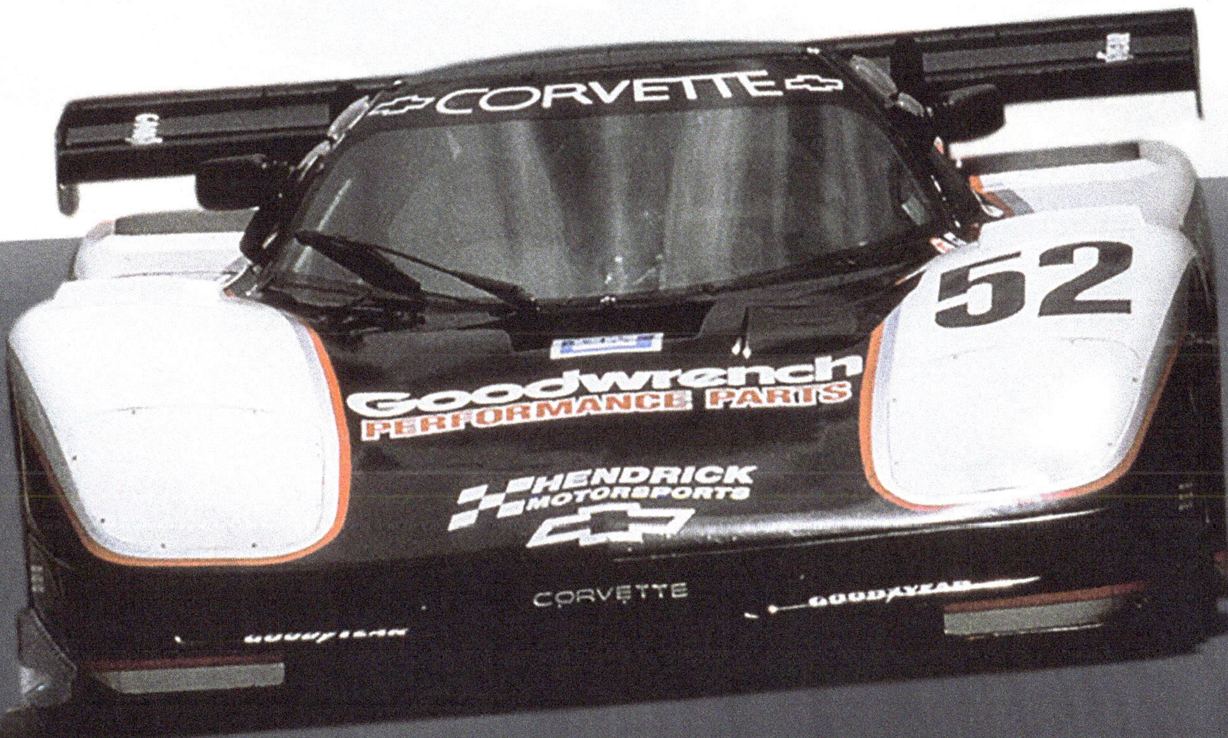

John Starkey

ACKNOWLEDGEMENTS

First of all to that Doyen of racecar restorers and dealers, Jack Boxstrom, who encouraged me to write this book. (And who also helped with his great knowledge of Corvette lore). Jack loves Corvettes, and has restored two of the John Greenwood "big block" Corvettes of the 1970s, besides racing many of the earlier, solid-axle fifties 'Vettes.

Dr. Dick Thompson, the "Racing Dentist," of early, solid-axle Corvettes, was kind enough to contribute his reminiscences of the early cars.

Steve Golden, who today owns two of the Greenwood cars, "Spirit of Le Mans," and "Spirit of Sebring, 76," was kind enough to contribute many of his own photographs for this book.

Next, thank you to Julie Fiegel of the GM Media Archive Center. Julie went to great lengths to supply us with many early (and later) shots of Corvettes being raced.

I spoke with as many of the drivers as possible, such as Orlando Costanzo, Jerry Thompson, Tony de Lorenzo, Bob Johnson, John Greenwood, Phil Curran, Elliott Forbes-Robinson, Javier Garcia, John Paul, Mike Brockman, Ron Grable, Rick Mancuso, Dennis McCosh, Walt Lister, Jim Crist, to get a flavor of what racing a Corvette in times gone by was like. It was obvious that, to a man, they had all loved racing the Corvette.

On the engineering side, Bill Tower contributed his memories of engineering the Stingray racecars, Ken Howes provided his experiences as the crew chief whilst racing the "Corvette GTP" car for the Hendricks team. Sarel van der Merwe, the team's chief driver, also remembered that car with affection.

Andy Pilgrim, the English driver for the GM Goodwrench team brought drivers' views of the C5-R up to the present with his experiences of racing at Daytona, Sebring and Le Mans, amongst other tracks. Thanks, Andy.

Mark Marabella, who today owns the ex-Walt Lister 396 Corvette provided photographs of the car as it is today. Mark loves driving his old "big block" 'Vette on the street.

Finally, to all those who have contributed information and whom I have not acknowledged, a big thank you. When the subject of a book on the racing career of the Corvette was mentioned, nearly every Corvette enthusiast had something to contribute.

ABOUT THE AUTHOR

JOHN STARKEY is a self-confessed racing fanatic, having written nineteen books on the subject, including *Ferrari 250 GT Tour de France*; *Lola T70, The Racing History*; *The Racing Porsches, R to RSR*; *Lola, The Illustrated History (Parts I & II)* with Ken Wells; *Ferrari – Fifty Years on the Track*; *Ferrari 166 to F50 GT – The Racing Berlinettas*; *930 to 935 – The Turbo Porsches*; and *Racing with a Difference – The History of IMSA*. John has owned and raced two Ferraris, a "Tour de France" Berlinetta and a Drogo-bodied 250GT Berlinetta, a Lola T70, a Porsche 935 and ex-IMSA March 84G. John is currently heavily involved in discovering the histories of old race cars.

TABLE OF CONTENTS

Foreword		vi
Introduction		ix
Chapter One	The Early Years 1953 to 1962	1
Chapter Two	The Sting Ray Era 1963 to 1967	37
Chapter Three	Mainly Big Blocks 1965 to 1983	53
Chapter Four	New Shape, New Beginning 1984 to 1996	111
Chapter Five	Drag Racing Corvettes	129
Appendix I	The Production Cars	139
Appendix II	Homologation Papers	151
Appendix III	Greenwood Papers	157
Appendix IV	Corvette Experimental Cars	175

DEDICATION

For everyone who has ever driven or raced a Corvette

and

For all the fans of Corvette Racing

FOREWORD

I was flattered when John Starkey asked me to write a foreword for this competition-oriented book about America's sports car. Besides being a well known driver of historic racing cars in both his native England and now on our side of the pond, John is a prolific author of special interest books about sporting automobiles. Also racing related, these now total some eight in number and cover such diverse marques as Porsche, Lola and Ferrari as well as his recent and widely acclaimed book about the post-war IMSA years in North America.

Chevrolet Corvette: the first four decades of racing sucess is a bit of a departure for John, since it covers both the racing and road version aspects of America's sports car but I'm sure you'll agree that this volume is all the better for its "dual purpose" aspect – just like the car itself.

My involvement with the marque began in my teens when a high school friend and I would frequently practice the art of liquefying the rear US Royals of his birthday present solid-axle car after school. Likely around this time, in 1958, I also attended my first sports car race at the Harewood Acres circuit, an ex-WW2 bomber base in Ontario, Canada, where I watched open mouthed as one Ed Leavens dusted sports car favorites like Porsches, Healeys and MGs with his vicious black '57 "Fuellie."

After reading *Road & Track* magazine's test of the 1957 version that extolled the "Performance at a Price" theme – a magazine road test concept that has continued unabated until today for the Corvette, I reluctantly sold my beloved MG TC which no longer seemed, well, even remotely adequate!

My own amateur road racing career began in 1961 and I haven't missed a year since, although my focus did switch from "contemporary" to "historic" in the early 1980s. While I couldn't afford a Corvette like Ed Leavens' '57 in the beginning, my historic Corvette racing involvement later made up for the lost horsepower.

A fuel injected '61 provided much fun and scary moments until I learned to disconnect the Factory optional rear anti-sway bar for certain circuits. After that, I managed to track down and restore the Dave Heinz "Rebel" Le Mans car as well as both the number 48 and number 50 John Greenwood Le Mans/IMSA/SCCA "Stars & Stripes" Big Block Stingrays. Later, another Greenwood Corvette joined the stable in the form of the "Spirit of Sebring" wide body 700hp monster that provided quite a contrast with the earlier little solid axle car and illustrated vividly how much the marque had evolved in just 15 years.

The announcement of the 1988 Corvette Challenge Series for 30 identically prepared cars, prompted the purchase of a brand new race-prepared coupe from our friendly local

Chevrolet dealer. Offering over a million dollars in prize money, the Challenge attracted a mix of enthusiastic amateurs like myself plus a dozen or more Pros desperate for the cash and the Series ability to promote and advance their careers. On track this proved a destructive combination – in my case transforming my beautiful Titanium number 6 coupe into a rough beater in a matter of months as it suffered major impacts at Dallas, Sears Point and Mosport – only one of which I could take credit for.

After the season's end final repairs, we put "old" number 6 back on the street for a year or two – a fun period of road work that perfectly illustrated the user friendly super car nature of the C-4 era 'Vettes. My "crew chief" Kathy often used it as her daily driver, the only complaint being the lengthy explanation as to the exact purpose of the 6 point roll cage in her shopping car to the grocery carry-out boys!

These days we only have one Corvette, a 1954 "Blue Flame" Six but, please, no laughing as I'll explain. Haven't you always loved the quirky design of the first Corvette – surely the last vestige of the Harley Earl years at the head of GM Styling, with its wide toothy grin, wire-mesh headlamp covers and cute little rocket pods on the rear fenders? Although the appearance promised much, the wimpy 6-banger, indifferent handling and the two speed Powerglide failed to deliver, exactly as in 1954 when buyers avoided the Chevy dealerships en masse, opting instead for the handling of an MG or the speed of a 4-gear Jaguar.

Today, however, armed with the power of hindsight, we know how to fix the problem. Duntov it – that's how! Now the blueprinted Blue Flame has 3 side draught Webers and the "Powerglide" apparition has been replaced by Zora's late '57 4-speed transmission. Optional 5.5" wheels from a '58, Pirelli 70 Series radials, HD springs and sway bars plus Koni shocks provide true period sports car handling, proving the old adage that it's never too late to have a happy childhood!

By now John will be reminding me this was only meant to be an intro and that I got a trifle carried away with my ownership reminiscences but that's the charm of this special and seductive marque. As a wrap-up, may I offer my own definitions of the uniqueness of America's favorite sports car?

Dual Purpose Character – Any Corvette, whether purchased in 1957 or 1996, could and can, if equipped with the right Factory options, be driven straight from the showroom to the race track where it has the potential to win, first time out. In 1957 we specified the fuel injected V8, HD brakes and suspension and the 4-speed transmission, likely hooked to a 4.11 gear. In 2002 it's even simpler – just buy a Z-06, bolt in the roll bar and go.

Adequate Power – A central theme of all five generations of Corvette, being in the range of 300 to approximately 650, depending on the production year. (We call it adequate, Nader said "excessive" – right on Ralph!)

Styling/Design – Always sensationally attractive but never mistaken for another brand. The indefinable "look" has endured through all its versions without diluting the solid Corvette personality.

Engineering – If not always on the cutting edge, at least at the forefront of GM's advanced engineering. Fiberglass body construction and fuel injection in the '50s, disc brakes and 4 wheel independent suspension in the mid-years and so on, right up to the present time.

Value for Money – Always an important trait of the Corvette. Even today a Z-06 coupe outperforms designer sports cars like Ferrari, Porsche and Aston Martin at roughly one-quarter to one-half the price.

Service – Not to be pedantic, but how many Ferrari dealers are there in your town? Exactly. Any Corvette goes to the local Chevrolet dealer where the necessary parts arrive the next day and the labor rates are the same as for your neighbor's mini van.

No wonder then that the Chevrolet Corvette soldiers on like an unstoppable energy bunny, larger than life and exhibiting such a strong persona that generations of corporate bean counters, a major gas crisis, periodic management indifference, economic recessions and repeated attacks by safety crusaders have not been able to derail it.

Like the American spirit, the Corvette is indomitable and will survive and prosper as long as refined petroleum product can be purchased out of a service station pump.

JACK C. BOXSTROM
March 2002

INTRODUCTION

It may sound strange, but as far as I can find, there have been very few books written about the Chevrolet Corvette in racing.

The Grand Sport has been well covered, particularly in Dave Friedman's book, but of the rest of the hundreds, maybe thousands, of Corvettes that have been raced in their fifty year history, very little is to be found in print about their exploits.

I first raced a Corvette in the late eighties. She was a 1965 coupe with a 350 cubic inch small block engine and I raced her at Spa, Monza and Brands Hatch. I didn't get a good practice at Spa and started way down the grid, somewhere around thirtieth if I remember right. I overtook twelve cars on the first lap and finished up, I think, seventh.

Boy, did that Corvette have grunt! It was when I arrived at corners that I found out the 'Vette's big drawback: Weight. Nimbleness was not a word applicable to the Corvette's handling. Still, I did like the beast. At Monza, with only five working cylinders (due to me over-revving the engine and breaking pushrods), we actually finished seventh as all the people in front of me fell off!

Later on, I had a street convertible '63 Stingray with outside pipes and knock-on wheels. Wonderful poser, that was. It would set off whole rows of auto burglar alarms with just one blast from the side-pipes.

Recently, I've had the 1976 Garcia Brothers Greenwood-style big block racer. The way that aluminum 477 cubic inch motor revs is astounding!

A friend lent me his 2000 model C5 coupe and I loved it on the street. Just why anyone would bother buying a modern Ferrari or Porsche streetcar, when you can buy the Corvette for less than a third of the price, is beyond me.

In this book, besides the story of the Corvette in the big International races, I've tried to capture the flavor of the many cars that were club raced and autocrossed. The guys who drove Corvettes in the local slalom or autocross on a Sunday are, to me, part of the whole fascinating story.

I hope you enjoy this history of the Corvette in racing. Chevrolet has a long and outstanding history in the Car World. The Corvette's racing history is a starring part in it.

JOHN STARKEY
March 2002

FRONT COVER PHOTOGRAPH:
The Corvette GTP, 1988.
[Photo: Courtesy of of Gordon Barrett.]

REAR COVER PHOTOGRAPHS:
Betty Skelton in the V8-engined 1956 Corvette at the
Daytona Speed Week in February 1956.
[Photo: Courtesy of GM Media Archives.]

Corvette Logo.
[Photo: Courtesy of GM Media Archives.]

BACKGROUND PHOTOGRAPH (PAGES iv TO ix):
Dick Gulstrand in his famous 1964 Corvette Sting Ray Roadster,
leads the pack at Laguna Seca.
[Photo: Courtesy of Dave Friedman.]

LIABILITY DISCLAIMER

The information in this book is distributed on an "as is" basis, without warranty. Much care has been taken in researching and compiling the information presented herein. However, neither the author nor Veloce Publishing make any representations or warranties with respect to the accuracy or completeness of the contents of this book, and specifically in regard to the implied valuation and authenticity, beyond the descriptions contained in the paragraphs of this book. The author and the publisher, Veloce Publishing, shall have no liability to any person or entity with respect to any liability, loss or damage caused, or alleged to be caused, directly or indirectly by the contents of this book. Neither the author nor the publisher shall be liable for any loss of profit or any other commercial damages, including but not limited to special, incidental, consequential or other damages.

CHAPTER ONE

THE EARLY YEARS
1953 to 1962

Daytona Speed Week, 1956. The flagman prepares Betty Skelton's Corvette for its record attempt.
[Photo: Used with permission of GM Media Archives.]

Daytona Speed Week, 1956. One of the three specially prepared V8 Corvettes races along the sand in front of an appreciative crowd in its search for records. [Photo: Used with permission of GM Media Archives.]

The Chevrolet Corvette is one of the few American cars to remain in continuous production since its inception in 1953. It is, arguably, America's most successful Sports/GT car ever. The Cobra and the Viper may have challenged its reign, but neither has been as long lasting as the Corvette.

THE BEGINNINGS – 1952 TO 1954

Way back in 1953, little or no thought was given by General Motors to racing their new Corvette. Indeed, "The General" saw the Corvette as merely something to persuade Americans away from the MGs and Jaguar XK120s that had been so successful in introducing Americans to sports cars in the postwar boom. We must, however, put this in perspective. There were only 11,000 sports cars of all makes registered in the United States in 1951, less than a quarter of a percent of that year's total new car registrations.

The story of the development of the original Corvette has been told many times. Briefly, the most astonishing thing about the gestation of the Corvette was the fact that Harley Earl, Head of the Styling Division at General Motors (although being a car enthusiast himself) was more interested in the use of fiberglass in other car bodies than in developing an all-new sports car. Ally this to the fact that Ed Cole, Chevrolet's Chief Engineer, wanted Chevrolet to have a new, "avant-garde" image and the stage was set for a new type of car to appear from Chevrolet.

To this end, in 1952, the management of the US Rubber Division of Naugatuck, Connecticut (makers of early fiberglass car bodies) were invited to General Motors in Detroit to show their "Alembic 1." This was a fiberglass-bodied full-sized Chevrolet convertible, and Naugatuck's representatives were to discuss with GM's management the possibility of a body for a two-seater convertible. Eventually, they lost out to a competitor when it came to producing the fiberglass bodies of the Corvette, but the fact that they were invited to tender for the contract shows that Chevrolet were serious about using this "different" material for their car bodies.

There were two projects that Harley Earl's team were engaged upon in 1952. One was a convertible in the usual Detroit tradition, the other a pure two-seat only sports car. Robert McLean, a graduate of the California Institute of Technology, oversaw the design of the first Corvette. He kept the old "Blue Flame" six-cylinder engine allocated to the new sports car as far back and down as possible, both to ensure a 50-50 weight distribution front to rear, and to lower the center of gravity as much as possible.

Maurice Olley designed the chassis frame and suspension in just ten days. Although it utilized many stock Chevrolet parts in the front suspension, the new car's rear suspension featured new parts, leaf springs were used to locate the rear axle, this with a differential ratio of 3.55:1. The new car's wheelbase came out at 102.0 inches, exactly the same as Jaguar's sensational XK120, several of which had been bought by General Motors to see what made them so special. Is it any coincidence that the (slightly) later 250 GT Ferrari would sport a wheelbase dimension just a third of an inch longer?

The old Chevrolet straight six engine of 253 cubic inches produced just 105 horsepower but Chevrolet's engineers gave it solid (instead of hydraulic) lifters, a high-lift camshaft, twin valve springs and uprated the compression from 7.5 to 8:1. Three Carter carburetors were used and this engine then gave 150bhp at 4,500rpm.

Where the transmission was concerned, Chevrolet eschewed a European-style manual transmission in favor of the Powerglide automatic gearbox. There simply hadn't been enough time in the car's development to design and produce a good manual gearbox.

Displayed at the Waldorf Astoria hotel in New York on January 17th, 1953 and then throughout America in the travelling Motorama show of early 1953, the new Corvette

The prototype Corvette of early 1953. Once its tour with the Motorama show was through, the prototype was used for several staged publicity shots, as seen here. Note the downward pointing fin of "Corvette" on the side molding. This and the exterior push-button door handles give away the fact that this is the prototype Corvette. [Photo: Courtesy of GM Archives.]

(named after a fast destroyer-like Navy ship) was enthusiastically received, and dealers were soon taking orders. Like many other special cars, however, the new Corvette was slow in getting into production, mainly due to difficulties encountered where the production of the new fiberglass body was concerned.

This had been contracted, finally, to the Molded Fiber Glass Body Company in Ashtabula, Ohio. The contract called for 12,300 bodies. No fewer than forty-six separate components went into each early body, and handling of the new material was to cause many a headache before Chevrolet became completely conversant with the material. After just fifteen cars had been produced, the assembly line was shifted from Flint, Michigan, to St. Louis in Missouri. By 1954, production had ground to a halt when sales dwindled rapidly as buyers found uneven build quality, and a car that was neither an out-and-out sports car nor a quiet cruiser.

As this book is dedicated to the racing history of the Corvette, we must note that not many seem to have been raced from these early years of production. Not surprising, really,

The first Corvette to be built at the new Flint, Michigan plant is proudly driven out of the door. Note the incorrect Bel Air wheel covers, which were put on the first twenty-five or so cars. [Photo: Courtesy of GM Archives.]

as they would have been placed in SCCA "C" Production class. There, they would have been up against the Mercedes-Benz 300SL Gullwing coupe, a car with better brakes

One driver who did try an early Corvette in national racing was Dr. Dick Thompson from Washington, DC, the "racing dentist" as the press named him. Bob Rosenthal lent an early, six-cylinder car to him to practice with at the Andrews Field races at Washington, D.C. in 1954. Thompson was then one of the leading lights in SCCA racing, having started with Porsches and now driving tuned Jaguar XK120s. Thompson later reported: "The Corvette was a six-cylinder Powerglide model with standard passenger car brakes and seatbelts. But, surprisingly, when I drove it in practice, the times were comparable to our Jaguar. Then the brakes heated and faded out. I kept punishing the Corvette and, by the end of the day, I had blown the rear seal out of the transmission as well. Regardless of the damage I had inflicted on the car, I was impressed and could see the potential."

One Corvette was entered in the 1954 Carrera Pan Americana race. In that mighty grind from the tip of Southern Mexico to the Mexican-American border, this car, like so many others, succumbed to engine maladies and failed to finish the race. Bill von Esser and Ernest Pultz, the brave crew, must take the honor of being the first people to enter a Corvette in an International event.

DUNTOV TO THE RESCUE – 1955 TO 1962

The big change that saw sales pick up was the introduction, on the new 1955 model, of Chevrolet's new and immortal 265 cubic inch "small block" V8, which produced some 195 bhp in an engine that weighed thirty pounds less than the old six cylinder engine it replaced.

The new small-block V8 had been inserted into a Corvette as early as late1953, under the direction of Mauri Rose, the three-times Indianapolis winner, who Chevrolet had hired as a performance consultant. Ed Cole, Chevrolet's Chief Engineer, first tested the V8 in the ex-Motorama prototype Corvette sometime in late fall, 1953. Mauri Rose immediately saw that, with Ford's introduction of its Thunderbird with a V8, the management of Chevrolet had no choice but to install a comparable V8, to satisfy the public demand for a more powerful car.

One man who was assigned to the Corvette engineering team at this time (May 1st, 1953) became its virtual Godfather and was to stay with it until his retirement, many years later. He was Zora Arkus-Duntov and his first job was to develop a new, high-lift camshaft that was allied to a 9.25:1 compression ratio. Two Carter four-barrel carburetors enabled the new engine to give 225 horsepower at 5,200rpm with 270lb/ft of torque at 3,000rpm. A three-speed manual transmission now became standard equipment and a new rear axle, with a 3.27:1 ratio as an option with the manual gearbox was fitted. The standard ratio of 3.55:1 was still available with the automatic gearbox.

This increased power and torque gave the Corvette a 0 to 60mph time of 7.5 seconds and the quarter mile could be covered in sixteen seconds with 90 plus mph being the terminal velocity. Not only was the V8 a more powerful engine than the old straight-six "Blue Flame" engine that it replaced, it was also forty-one pounds lighter. This helped bring the weight distribution of the Corvette to 52/48 front to rear and helped improve the handling, along with the changes that Duntov now initiated in this department.

Daytona Speed Week, February 1956. Zora Arkus-Duntov's Corvette streaks along the beach. Duntov, John Fitch and Betty Skelton drove the three cars to record speeds. [Photo: Used with permission of GM Media Archives.]

Duntov had seen that the Corvette's handling did not match up to the horsepower that now propelled his re-vamped Corvette. He set about using his previous road-racing experience to cure the car's handling problems. Shims were inserted between the chassis and the front crossmember to increase the castor angle of the front suspension by two degrees. More shims were used to alter the angle of the steering idler arm, to reduce the roll oversteer inherent in the front suspension design.

At the rear, the rear spring hangers were changed, making the bow of the rear springs more even and removing the roll understeer that the previous design had exhibited. After these changes had been made, Zora Arkus-Duntov test drove the Corvette and reported that: "The car goes where it is pointed, and does so without hesitation. On turns taken hard, it does not plow or skid, but gets into a drift. If the right amount of power is fed in, the drift can be maintained without danger of the rear end getting presumptuous and assuming the position of the front."

Betty Skelton sitting in one of the specially prepared Corvettes used in the 1956 Daytona Speed Week at rest.
[Photo: Used with permission of GM Media Archives.]

Duntov took a disguised 1956 Corvette to the Pike's Peak hillclimb on September 9th, 1955 and set a record of 17 minutes, 24.05 seconds in the stock car class.

Shortly after this, Duntov took an old 1954 Corvette, equipped with the V8 engine, to Phoenix, where GM had their Proving Grounds, a gently-banked Oval circuit. He had had this car fitted with a small windshield and a fin, "a la" D type Jaguar, besides taping off the radiator opening to reduce drag at high speed.

Duntov had further developed a new camshaft so that the engine would give 250bhp on some very special models. He had worked out that he needed a further thirty-five to forty horsepower to reach 150mph and thus the re-designed camshaft. His new camshaft enabled the old "mule" Corvette to reach 163mph, as the engine now revved to 6500rpm before valve-bounce intruded.

In December, Duntov and a back-up team of engineers, took this Corvette to Daytona Beach to try for the magic 150mph on the flat sands. With a Corvette equipped with one of

Betty Skelton, in one of the 1956 Corvettes, prepares for the measured mile. [Photo: Used with permission of GM Media Archives.]

Left: Another view of one of the three 1956 Corvettes at the Daytona Speed Week in February 1956. [Photo: Used with permission of GM Media Archives.]

these more powerful engines, Duntov reached over 150mph on the beach at Daytona during January in 1956. The Standing Mile record was taken at 89.363mph. John Fitch drove an SR Corvette (Sports Racing) and set the Flying Mile record at 145.543mph.

From 1956, the production Corvette, as the V8 powered sports/GT car that we know today, was up and running. It should be said that the 1956-57 single-headlight Corvette is a

Below: Betty Skelton in the "Production" Corvette pace car during the 1956 Daytona Speed Week. [Photo: Used with permission of GM Media Archives.]

Betty Skelton posing in front of a 1956 Corvette. Note that she is wearing her aviatrix's helmet. In the speed run itself, she wore a helmet loaned to her by Mauri Rose, three times Indianapolis 500 winner. [Photo: Used with permission of GM Media Archives.]

very pure body design, particularly for an American car of the period when fins, fake scoops and such were all the rage. Like most cars of the fifties, Corvettes suffered from inadequate braking but this was only because the old drum brakes were nearing the end of their useful life as performance increased and the new disc brake was set to take over in the near future.

In February, at the Daytona Speed Week, Duntov and John Fitch, noted American road racer and an ex-World War II fighter pilot, were back again, this time accompanied by Betty Skelton, an aerobatics pilot. Fitch and Skelton also posted good speeds, 145.543 and 137.773 mph respectively. (Apart from being a pilot, Betty Skelton was also an advertising spokesperson for Chevrolet and Dodge.)

The Corvette that Duntov used for this record attempt was actually the old 1954 "mule" car, now fitted with 1956-style front and rear bodywork and a plastic tonneau cover. It had also been fitted with experimental cylinder heads, which gave the engine a compression ratio of 10.3:1. Power was whispered at 255bhp. With this Corvette, Duntov achieved 150.583mph.

The 1957 SS, developed by Duntov for racing. Note the prominent "Fuel Injection" badge on the side.
[Photo: 2001 General Motors Corporation. Used with permission of GM Media Archives.]

In 1957, Chevrolet took their new, fuel injected Corvette to Daytona to try for speed records. Sat between a new '57 Chevy and the course car, the enclosed cockpit Corvette SR-2 certainly looked the part. [Photo: 2001 General Motors Corporation. Used with permission of GM Media Archives.]

Only one month later, four Corvettes were entered for the 1956 running of the Sebring 12-Hour race and John Fitch was contracted to prepare and manage the team. The cars had been entered under the banner of a Chevrolet dealer, Raceway Enterprises of Dundee, Illinois, in order to disguise the fact that they were a factory effort. Still, not too many people were fooled!

Three cars were equipped with the Duntov camshaft, two four-barrel carburetors and ported manifolds. One experimental car used a four-speed ZF gearbox and had the engine bored out to the class limit of five liters (307 cubic inches). All the Corvettes had big fuel tanks, Halibrand magnesium wheels and extra driving lights. Walt Hansgen and John Fitch finished ninth overall and won the Sports class C modified category and the next Corvette finished in fifteenth place overall. Considering the superiority of European racing sports cars during this period, this was not a bad result. Sadly, in April, Duntov rolled a Corvette that he was testing and broke a vertebra in his back, putting him out of action until June.

Duntov had also prepared a C-production roadster for Dick Thompson in 1956 for SCCA events, and Thompson's success in winning his class allowed Duntov to convince Chevrolet's top brass that he should be allowed to develop the Corvette further. In later years, Thompson remembered: "John Fitch had been asked by Chevrolet to race a Corvette in SCCA races in 1956, but he was already committed to driving a D type Jaguar for Briggs Cunningham. John recommended me and so I got the job."

"Chevrolet sold me a Corvette at a very reasonable price, supplied parts and a mechanic and took the car back after each race to evaluate it."

The night before Thompson's first race, held at Laguna Seca, Frank Burrell, a Chevrolet engineer, put in new 'Cerametalix' brake linings in an attempt to help the Corvette's weak point, its brakes. Thompson's Corvette also had twin four-barrel carburetors, which had a tendency to flood; Burrell cured this problem, too.

Thompson was gridded sixth but by the end of the first lap was leading the race! Although he held on to the end, the brakes had completely gone away by the last lap and Tony Settember in a Mercedes 300SL took the win, leaving Thompson in second place. With Chevrolet's engineers concentrating on the Corvette, Thompson won the next two races at Beverly and Seafair.

The fuel injection, four-speed gearbox and RPO 684-specification suspension and brakes were developed during the 1956 season, which really turned the Corvette into a credible racing machine. The RPO 684 specification comprised stronger springs, a stiffer anti-roll bar, quicker steering ratio (the steering lock was reduced from 3.5 turns lock to lock to 2.9), heavy-duty shock absorbers, a Positraction (limited-slip) differential and finned brake drums with vented back plates plus the aforementioned 'Cerametalix' brake linings. Amongst

February 7th, 1957. A mechanic tends to Bill Mitchell's SR-2 Corvette on Daytona Beach in 1957 for an attempt to garner speed records. Notice not only the enclosed cockpit but also the wheel discs and headlamp covers, all an attempt to reduce drag. With Buck Baker driving, the SR-2 took the standing mile record at 93.047 mph and the flying mile at 152.866 mph. [Photo: 2001 General Motors Corporation. Used with permission of GM Media Archives.]

The start of practice for the Sebring 12-Hours in 1956. Ahead of the Corvette, which was driven to 9th overall, first in class, by John Fitch and Walt hansgen, can be seen Lotus 11's (one driven by Colin Chapman himself), a Kurtis Roadster, a Ford Thunderbird and Ferraris out front. [Photo: 2001 General Motors Corporation. Used with permission of GM Media Archives.]

others who won in 1956 Corvettes with these options fitted to their Corvettes were Norm Munson, Bark Henry and Fred Windridge.

Again with Sebring in mind, Duntov built a Corvette "special" in May, featuring a longer nose and a tailfin. This was the SR-2 and Curtis Turner and Dr. Dick Thompson gave it several good outings in races. One such victory was at the Pikes Peak hillclimb, where

The GT class winners at Sebring in 1957 (for cars of over five liters capacity) were Dr. Dick Thompson and Gaston Andrey in their factory-entered Corvette. [Photo: 2001 General Motors Corporation. Used with permission of GM Media Archives.]

Dr. Dick Thompson set a new record for a production car in 1956. Called the "Purple People eater," after the then-current hit song (and painted purple) this SR-2 won the 1958 SCCA Class B Championship with Jim Jeffords as the driver.

Recalling that period, Dick Thompson recalled: "That Corvette was really pretty good, except that it wouldn't stop! I had several accidents due to the brakes, or rather, the lack of them. I had to set the 'Vette up so that I could dirt track it around, to scrub the speed off."

The Jim Jeffords entry at the 1958 Sebring race was not a stock Corvette but was the ex-Jerry Earl SR-2 (Sebring Racer), chassis number E56S002522. This car, the first of the three built, came about because Jerry Earl (who had been racing a Ferrari) was provided with the SR-2 by his father, Harley Earl. It probably didn't sit too well that a GM Vice President's son was not racing a GM product!

The SR2 had first been delivered to Jerry Earl as a stock Corvette. In May 1956, Earl took it to the Chevrolet Research and Development Center, where it was modified with parts developed for the Sebring racers. Apart from the new bodywork with the curious dorsal fin on the rear deck, the SR-2 featured an almost stock twin-carburetor engine and three-speed transmission, although this probably didn't last long before being uprated to fuel injection and a four-speed transmission. What is certain is that Earl took the car back to the R&D Center some time in 1956, to have modifications made to it that had been suggested to him by Dr. Dick Thompson. Certainly, by early 1957, Smokey Yunick had bored and stroked the Chevy V8 in Bill Mitchell's SR-2 (the second SR-2 built) to 336 cubic inches, and equipped it also with fuel injection and the four-speed transmission.

Mitchell's Corvette also possessed a track three inches wider than standard and the engine was mounted further back and over to the passenger side in the chassis. A 45-gallon fuel tank gave Mitchell's SR-2 extraordinary range. After Mitchell had "mothballed" his SR-2 in 1958, the car was bought by Don Yenko, who carried on racing the old Corvette into the early '60s.

In December 1956, Jerry Earl entered his SR-2 at the Nassau Trophy Races with Curtis Turner nominated as the driver. The Corvette won its first race but then went off-track in the next race and was retired.

Duntov experimented with another variant based on the Corvette in 1957, the Sebring SS. This model had a tube frame chassis, magnesium body and a De Dion rear axle. This was a project designated the XP-64.

Someone else who bought a 1956 Corvette was Dick Gulstrand, later to become a very important part of Chevrolet's racing efforts: "I had bought a 1954 Corvette but didn't really like it. Then I bought a '56 model and became friendly with Zora Arkus-Duntov. He helped me get the right parts such as fuel injection and the Cerametalix brakes and the right springs. I started racing the car in 1958 and right away, it handled well."

"I was an aerospace engineer by trade and had started out racing sprint cars and midgets but too many people got killed and as I had friends racing Jags and Healeys in road racing, I went to a few events. I really like it, so I turned to road racing. This seemed to me to be a much more gentlemanly form of racing!"

Bill Mitchell's XP-87 Sting Ray Race car. In this photograph of the car in later years, it is accompanied by a 1957 SR-2 and a Grand Sport Corvette. There were three SR-2s built, one going to Bill Mitchell, another to Harley Earl's son Jerry and the third went to Harlow Curtis, the GM President. This latter car was very much a street car, however. [Photo: 2001 General Motors Corporation. Used with permission of GM Media Archives.]

"Suddenly, on the West Coast, lots of tracks sprang up. There was Riverside, Pomona, Willow Springs, Torrey Pines. Although I was living out of a suitcase, it was a lot of fun."

A notable "first" for the 1957 Corvette was the addition of "Ramjet" fuel injection added to the 283 cubic inch V8. "Fuelies" (as they have come to be known) were the fastest of the Corvettes at this time. The fuel injection by Rochester was claimed to help the V8 engine produce 283bhp at 6,200rpm. Problems with maintenance of the injection kept down sales of this 1957 car to only 240, but they gave a 0 to 60mph time of just 6.5 seconds and have become one of the most collectible of all old Corvettes.

In 1957, for the first time, a Corvette could be ordered with a four-speed gearbox. With this, and the lowest rear axle ratio available (4.11 to 1), a 1957 "fuelie" could record 0 to 60mph in 5.5 seconds, and still go on to pull a maximum speed in excess of 130mph.

In February 1957, the Corvette was seen again at the Daytona Speed Week. Paul Goldsmith's Corvette turned 91.301mph to win the production class standing start mile. Bill Mitchell's SR-2, now with an engine rated at 310 horsepower, was also there and, with Buck Baker driving, the enclosed cockpit Corvette took the standing mile record in the modified class at 93.047mph, and the flying mile at 152.866mph.

A 1959 Corvette Roadster leads an A C Ace and another similar Corvette in a race probably in the early 1960s. [Photo: Used with permission of GM Media Archives.]

For the 1957 running of the Sebring 12 hours, four "normal" Corvettes, with their hardtops affixed to qualify them for the GT Production class, were entered and Dick Thompson, partnered by Gaston Andrey, won their class as well as placing 12th overall. Dale Duncan, Jim Jeffords and John Kilborn in the number 3 Corvette placed second in class, 15th overall. The next finisher in the class was a Mercedes 300SL, but the Corvettes

A 1959 Corvette Convertible leads an MGA and an Elva Courier in this race in Maryland, circa 1960.
[Photo: Used with permission of GM Media Archives.]

Zora Arkus-Duntov could not help but try to develop cars for GM to race with. Here he is with Cerv-1, a single-seater that he designed and had built in 1960. [Photo: Used with permission of GM Media Archives.]

beat it by twenty laps. On top of this superb result, the SR-2 finished in 16th place, winning the Modified Production class. Duntov's "Sebring SS" had been tried in practice by such luminaries as Juan Manuel Fangio and Stirling Moss who commented favorably but in the race proper, it lasted just twenty three laps, before dropping out with suspension problems.

The gestation and reasoning behind this "Sports-prototype" SS are interesting and bear recounting. Duntov had quickly realized that, whilst the "standard" Corvette (with a little tuning help!) was a good bet in the long-distance endurance races in the GT class, there was no way in which it could be competitive with, say, a Jaguar D type or a Ferrari 290, 335S or Maserati 300S.

We need to backtrack a little. Harley Earl, GM's Chief Stylist, had bought a Jaguar D Type in the late spring of 1956. His idea was to substitute a Chevrolet V8 for the Jaguar straight six engine and, together with some styling modifications (including swapping it over

Two 1961 Corvettes line up for a race at Virginia International Raceway, Circa 1962. [Photo: Used with permission of GM Media Archives.]

to left-hand drive), race it as a "Chevrolet Corvette." Zora Arkus-Duntov quickly came up with an alternative plan, for Chevrolet to build their own in-house sports-racer. The project was approved and the result, "Project XP-64" or "SS," was put into motion.

With time running out before the 1957 season began, there was not time to build a team and, therefore, only one car was made. To save time, a Mercedes 300SL road car was used as a study for the SS's chassis. The final item, though only nominally similar to the 300SL's chassis, weighed just 180 pounds. Wheelbase was just 92 inches.

Suspension was by coil-over shock absorbers all round, with hand-made A-arms at the front. A de Dion axle was used to transmit the drive from the transmission to the rear wheels. For brakes, Duntov used the largest drums possible, a full twelve inches in diameter and two and a half inches wide. The rear ones were mounted inboard and a Halibrand

Marvin Panch and George Robertson shared this basically stock Corvette in the 1962 running of the Daytona 24-Hour race and came in third in their class. [Photo: 2001 General Motors Corporation. Used with permission of GM Media Archives.]

Robert Johnson failed to finish in this Corvette at Daytona in 1962, but the Ferrari ace, Olivier Gendebien, drove the Ferrari 250 GT SWB seen behind it to 16th overall and third in class. [Photo: 2001 General Motors Corporation. Used with permission of GM Media Archives.]

quick-change rear end was fitted to aid gear changes in the pits. A sophisticated proportioning valve was used in conjunction with a brake servo to spread the braking power out evenly and avoid rear-wheel lock up.

The 283 cubic inch small block engine had aluminum heads and Rochester fuel injection, whilst the compression ratio was kept down to 9:1 to let the engine last Sebring's twelve hours of racing. This engine was rated at 307 bhp at 6400 rpm. With magnesium-alloy bodywork mounted, the SS weighed just 1,850 pounds, a commendable effort, as the Jaguar D type weighed nearly 2000 pounds, as did most of the Ferrari and Maserati opposition.

Sadly, all the effort went to waste as the car was only just completed in time for Sebring and numerous faults arose in practice, not least being the heat generated within the car that fried the drivers, John Fitch and Piero Taruffi. A "Mule," bodied in fiberglass, had already been built and tested, and the fiberglass body did not transmit the heat the way the magnesium-alloy body of the racecar did. The car, whilst showing great promise in the early stages, was retired with myriad small problems and then was never raced again, due to the AMA ban on racing

Here is Robert Johnson again at Daytona in 1962. The little Porsche 718RS61 behind him was driven by Peter Da Costa and took sixth overall and second in class. [Photo: 2001 General Motors Corporation. Used with permission of GM Media Archives.]

1962 Daytona 24-Hours. Jack Knab finished fifth in class in the number 75 Corvette, whilst Dick Rathmann and Harry Heuer gain on it in their Chaparral, which finished sixth overall and second in class. The Lotus Elite was thirtieth and fifth in class.
[Photo: 2001 General Motors Corporation. Used with permission of GM Media Archives.]

introduced in June 1957. It did, however, record a top speed of 183mph during testing at the Phoenix GM proving grounds in December 1958, and Duntov drove the car at over 150mph in February 1959 on the banking at the Daytona Speedway's official opening.

Dick Thompson took a Corvette, fitted with all the performance options Chevrolet could supply, and won the newly created B-Production class in 1957. After winning at Sebring,

Jack Knab again, this time with Bob Holbert's class-winning Porsche 718RSK overtaking, hotly pursued by the fifth-place-finishing Ferrari 250 Testa Rossa of George Constantine. [Photo: Used with permission of GM Media Archives.]

with co-driver Gaston Andrey, Thompson won at Road America, Virginia International Raceway and Cumberland, besides placing well in the other races that comprised the Championship. Thompson called the 1957 Corvette: "The best racing Corvette ever." The SCCA's Class B Sports racing Championship was won by J. E. Rose in a Corvette.

Jim Jeffords and Fred Windridge took their Corvette to Venezuela for the Grand Prix in November of 1957 but were out with overheating in just thirty-one laps. This was the ex-Jerry Earl SR-2, which Jeffords ran as part of Chicago's Nicky Racing Team.

Jim Rathmann, later to win the Indianapolis 500 of 1960, co-drove a 1957 "Fuelie" Corvette, together with Dick Douane in the 1958 Sebring 12-Hours and, again, the 1957

Duncan Black and M. R. J. Wylie shared this 1962 Corvette to win their class at Sebring in 1962. [Photo: 2001 General Motors Corporation. Used with permission of GM Media Archives.]

Corvette won the GT class. Jim Rathmann remembered: "I drove so many cars. Let's see – Oh, yes, this was the car that belonged to Dick Douane. That was a heavy car, fitted with Rochester fuel injection, but we were the fastest car at night. We had no real problems with the car although Dick was in a 'touring' mode and the car would drift back through the pack

In the pits, prior to the 1962 running of the Sebring 12-Hours, the number two car gets attention. [Photo: 2001 General Motors Corporation. Used with permission of GM Media Archives.]

when he drove and then I'd climb in and push the car back to the front. Afterwards, a couple of guys were mad at me 'cos they wouldn't get out of the way. They were driving in the middle of the track when I came to overtake them. They didn't understand that I was a pro and driving for money, so I body slammed them and they didn't like that!"

One of the other Corvettes racing at Sebring in 1962. This one, driven by Jerry Grant and Pat Pigott, retired just before the finish when the fuel pump failed. The little Alfa Romeo Guilette SV behind it also retired. This was driven by Walter Ballard and Charlie Rainville. Charlie Rainville later became IMSA's first Tech. Inspector.
[Photo: 2001 General Motors Corporation. Used with permission of GM Media Archives.]

Le Mans 24-Hours, 1960. John Fitch and Bob Grossman drove this Briggs Cunningham-entered Corvette to eighth place overall and took victory in the 3 to 5 liter GT class. [Photo: Courtesy of The Klemantaski Collection.]

Incidentally, Troy Ruttman's brother, Bert Ruttman, another Indianapolis speedway driver, used a 1957 Corvette to win a production car race at Pomona in heavy rain in February 1958, proving that the Corvette wasn't only a 'dry-weather' racer. It also proved that Indianapolis racers could drive in the wet!

At that same Sebring 12-Hour race, Dick Thompson took his 1957 Corvette, partnered by Fred Windridge and "Honest" John Kilborn, to second in the class.

Once again, a Corvette won its class at the Pikes Peak hillclimb. During this period, Corvettes won virtually everywhere in America, Jim Jeffords winning the 1958 and 1959 B-Production SCCA Championship in the "Purple People Eater" (really Jerry Earl's old SR-2).

Duntov's next experimental Corvette was far more successful. This was the Stingray, really the prototype of the Corvette of 1963 that bore the same name. Bill Mitchell designed this special on the SS that had been used for practice at Sebring (the "Mule" SS's chassis) and it was built in late 1958. Dick Thompson raced it in SCCA events in 1959 and 1960. Thompson won the C-Sports category in 1960, despite several accidents with the car. "That really was an excellent chassis" recounted Thompson later; "With proper development, it could have formed the foundation for a World-class race car." (A little-known fact is that Bill Mitchell believed in this Stingray racer so much, he put his own money into supporting Thompson to race the car. Larry Shinoda, the Stingray's designer, worked as Thompson's mechanic at each race.)

The Stingray was up against such heavyweight opposition as Porsche RSKs, Lister-Jaguars and Chevrolets, but by mid-season 1959, Shinoda and Thompson had the Stingray working well and won the next year's Championship. Later on, in 1962, Bill Mitchell used the Stingray as his personal transportation, trying a variety of modifications that would later on show up on production cars. The 377 cubic inch, and later on the 427 cubic inch engine both made their debuts in this car.

In 1960, apart from winning the SCCA C Sports Racing and B National Production classes, Corvettes won again at Sebring, Bill Fritts and Chuck Hall bringing their car home to win the up to five liter GT class and finish in sixteenth place overall.

At the Le Mans 24-Hours one (out of three entered) of Briggs Cunningham's white and blue Corvettes placed eighth overall and first in the four-five liter class at Le Mans (John Fitch and Bob Grossman driving). This Corvette was timed at 151 mph down the long Mulsanne straight.

Foreshadowing the next generation of Sting Ray Corvettes was the XP-700 "Shark" show car that Bill Mitchell introduced onto the show circuit in 1961. The lines of the 1963 Sting Ray were easily visible in this car, soon to be re-named the "Mako Shark."

In 1961 it was the turn of Dale Morgan and Delmo Johnson to win the GT class at Sebring, something that Corvettes were making a habit of. Dick Thompson won the B-Production Championship in this year, as well as Corvettes winning A and B Production SCCA titles in 1962. Thompson's Corvette was a new one that belonged to Grady Davis, a director of Gulf Oil and soon to sponsor the Ford GT40s with John Wyer as his team manager.

Thompson was literally showered with goodies, the resources of Gulf Oil giving him the best of several engines tried for each race and the gearing being selected appropriately for each track. Thompson and the Gulf Oil-prepared Corvette won eight consecutive races to win the title.

Another notable Corvette racer who started his career in 1961 was Jerry Thompson: "I started racing Corvettes with a 1956 car that I had bought in 1960. To begin with, this 'Vette was strictly stock, with a single carburetor and a three-speed transmission. I was a development engineer at Chevrolet for twelve years and Duntov was very good to me, helping me with parts. By the time I sold the car two years later, it had been equipped with fuel injection and a four-speed transmission. That was a very good car, but then I went from the sublime to the ridiculous, buying and racing a Lotus Super 7! I tried to buy a ZO6 Stingray from Chevrolet and had two people at GM trying to help me get it but I failed. I later heard that that car had been sent to the crusher. Such a shame."

In 1962, Dick Thompson won the A-production SCCA Championship, this time using a 1962 Corvette, fitted with the bigger 327 cubic inch small block motor. Thompson had helped to develop this engine as the test driver. Duntov sent three cars fitted with the new engine to Sebring and Thompson drove each one until something broke. Then he would repeat the same drill with the next car, and the next. By that time, the Chevrolet engineers would have the first car ready to go again. In this way, any problems with the new 327 engine were ironed out before production began.

Don Yenko was the winning driver in B Production in 1962 and he repeated the trick in 1963. Apart from these National Championships, Corvettes won their class at the Daytona Continental and the Three Hours of Riverside.

At Sebring in 1962, the habit of winning the GT class was maintained, Duncan Black and M. R. J. Wylie, coming in eighteenth overall to claim the over four liter GT class.

Frank Dominiana took the B Production Championship in 1964 but that was the end for these "early" Corvettes. Carroll Shelby's A.C. Cobra, fully a thousand pounds lighter than the Corvette, had appeared and trounced the Corvettes. The Corvette, apart from the Grand Sport adventure, would have to wait until 1968 before it was a serious racing threat again.

Chapter Two

THE STING RAY ERA
1963 to 1967

The new Sting Ray Corvette in action on a racetrack. [Photo: Used with permission of GM Media Archives.]

The Sting Ray, pretty much an all-new Corvette, came from a project dubbed XP-720 built in 1959. This car was loosely based upon the design of the racing Stingray mentioned in the previous chapter. The stunning new Jaguar E-type also saw the light of day in 1960 and Bill Mitchell was an early buyer of one of these and admired its beautiful lines. Mitchell very much wanted to produce America's answer to the E-type Jaguar and, to a great extent with the Sting Ray, he succeeded.

New Beginnings – 1963 to 1967

Apart from the body shape, the new Sting Ray featured (like the E-type Jaguar) an independent rear suspension of the three-link type with radius rods. This used an unorthodox method of springing, a single transverse leaf spring, as there was not enough room for coil springs. The brakes were still drums, but were now self-adjusting. In hindsight, it seems odd that Jaguar had introduced the disc brake on their XK150 in 1958, yet the Corvette was still using an outmoded method of retardation as late as 1964. Where the chassis was concerned, the new Sting Ray Corvette still employed what was essentially a box section ladder frame.

The Sting Ray used that classic amongst the small block Chevrolet family, the 327 cubic inch engine. With fuel injection fitted, 375bhp was claimed, taking the new Sting Ray from 0 to 100mph in just 15 seconds.

The 1964 Sting Ray was very similar to the 1963 model, the most noticeable difference being the deletion of the divided rear window in the coupe model, as too many customers had not seen the lurking police car hidden by the strip! The fake hood louvers were also deleted, whilst the extractor vents behind the windows were now made functional.

For 1965, the side front fender louvers were redesigned and opened, which allowed them to duct heat out of the engine department. The standard hood had no trim and no depressions. Mechanically, 1965 saw the biggest change to the engine line-up for the Corvette. The new big block engine had arrived, first of all with a capacity of 396 cubic inches and rated at 425 horsepower. It took a compression ratio of 11:1 to achieve this power and required premium fuel to cope with this. To handle the extra power, the 1965 big block Corvette had a heavier clutch fitted together with a larger radiator and fan. In the suspension department, there were stiffer front springs to cope with the extra weight of the big block engine (650 lbs), a thicker front anti-roll bar and a new rear anti-roll bar.

The biggest breakthrough in 1965 was the use of disc brakes. Four piston calipers were used on each wheel and this greatly improved the stopping power of the relatively heavy Corvette. 1965 also saw the end of the availability of fuel injection on the production cars.

Two of the new Sting Ray Corvettes battle it out in Maryland, closely followed by a Morgan. [Photo: Used with permission of GM Media Archives.]

The 1966 and 1967 models were very similar to the 1965 car, the differences being mainly trim and a new square mesh style cast grille. This was also the first year for the big block 427 cubic inch engine, which necessitated a new hood design to accommodate the higher engine. The performance of the new big block Corvette was shattering: 0 to 60 mph achievable in just 4.8 seconds, in a car geared for a maximum speed of 140 miles an hour.

One of the first drivers to race a Sting Ray in competition was Tony de Lorenzo: "My brother and I (I was twenty-one at the time) convinced my Dad to order a really trick Corvette as a company car. Shortly after we'd put the order in, Duntov called us. He wanted to know exactly what we were going to use the car for. Finally, I told him that I was going to use it in drivers' school. That was all he wanted to know. When we got that car, it was

A 1963 split window coupe being raced in SCCA 'A' Production. [Photo: Courtesy of GM Media Archives.]

Dick Gulstrand was one of the best of the Corvette racers of the early '60s. At Laguna Seca, he exchanges some last words with his mechanic before the start of an SCCA race. Behind him on the left is a Lotus Cortina, on the right an Elva Courier. [Photo: Courtesy of Dave Friedman.]

The 1962 Grand Sport Corvette. [Photo: 2001 General Motors Corporation. Used with permission of GM Media Archives.]

pretty spectacular – I'm sure Duntov had his engine guys give it some special attention, as that engine went really well."

"The car was delivered to us with scrubbed Goodyear Blue Streaks on it. In later years, I realized that meant that the car must have been checked out on the skid pad, at the very least!"

During this period, as we have observed, the Shelby Cobra was beating the Corvettes on the race track and, in an attempt to beat the Cobra, the "Big Block" Chevrolet engine of, first 396 and then 427 cubic inches was introduced in 1965 and 1966 respectively.

Another shot of the 1962 Corvette Grand Sport. [Photo: 2001 General Motors Corporation. Used with permission of GM Media Archives.]

In 1966, a 427 cubic inch Corvette was tested by Sports Car Graphic and did the 0 to 100 mph dash in 11.2 seconds, with a top speed of 140 mph.

Back in 1962, on October 14th, both the new Shelby A.C. Cobra and the Sting Ray made their racing debut at the Riverside Three Hour Enduro. Bill Krause in the Shelby Cobra

The grid for the 5-lap race, which was held before the Nassau Trophy Race in December 1963. Dr. Dick Thompson drove Grand Sport number 80, whilst Jim Hall, the constructor and driver (with Hap Sharp) of the Chaparrals, drove another Grand Sport (number 65). Roger Penske drove the number 50 Grand Sport. Next to Dick Thompson is the 289 Cobra driven by John Everly, whilst Augie Pabst stands on the right. He was driving the new Lola Mark 6 GT, whose tail is just visible on the right. This, the forerunner of the Ford GT40, would win both this race and the Nassau Trophy. Pity the poor Volvo P1800 on the left of the front row! [Photo: 2001 General Motors Corporation. Used with permission of GM Media Archives.]

Riverside and a 1963 Corvette Coupe keeps ahead of a 1962 Roadster as they come onto the pit straight. [Photo: Courtesy of GM Media Archives.]

pulled out a handsome lead on the new Corvette, driven by Dave McDonald and it was easy to see that the new Corvette was not competitive against the Cobra. A thousand extra pounds of weight ensured that the Corvette would be beaten by the lighter Cobra.

Duntov then conceived a "Super Corvette" to beat the Shelby Cobras and it was called the Grand Sport. One hundred and twenty-five of these Grand Sports were planned

Opportunity lost. The 1963 Corvette Grand Sport. If only Chevrolet's management had allowed them to be built as a run of the 125 planned, it is doubtful if Ferrari's famed GTO would have beaten them. [Photo: 2001 General Motors Corporation. Used with permission of GM Media Archives.]

to be built in 1963, in order to homologate them into the Production GT car class. At the last moment, Chevrolet management realized that this Grand Sport would violate their "no racing" agreement with the other major factories and the project was cancelled, after which just five cars were built from the parts already amassed. And what a car!

Although the basic chassis layout was still a "ladder" frame, round, seamless steel tubing instead of the more usual rectangular steel tubing was used. This gave greater strength than the normal production chassis. Whilst following the production car in its suspension layout, every item was hand-made to lighten it and increase its durability. The Grand Sport was also just 7/8ths the size of the production car. The gas tank held thirty-six and a half gallons of fuel and the body was thinner than the normal Sting Ray. Weight was down at 2000 pounds.

Originally, Duntov had meant to put the aluminum 377 cubic inch, twin-plug 500bhp-plus engine into the Grand Sport but the prototype received the 327 small block, although in highly tuned configuration, which gave some 360bhp. With this, Masten Gregory lapped Sebring close to the lap record and those present at the test realized that victory in 1963 was within their grasp.

A 1964 production Sting Ray Corvette Coupe running in "B" Production SCCA class at the Daytona Speedway. [Photo: Used with permission of GM Media Archives.]

Above: A typical scene at a Southern California autocross in the late Sixties. Stingray Corvettes line up to take their turn. [Photo: Courtesy of Mark Marabella.]

Left: Dick Gulstrand in action in his 1964 Corvette. Behind him is the nemesis of most Corvettes, a Porsche. This one is a 904. Notice that Gulstrand has a roller skate strapped on to his roll bar. This was in reference to when Dick inadvertently rolled a Corvette. [Photo: Courtesy of Dave Friedman.]

Two Grand Sports, chassis numbers 003 and 004, were lent, respectively, to Chevrolet dealer Dick Douane and Gulf Oil executive Grady Davis. Davis hired Dick Thompson to drive his, whilst Douane planned to drive his own car. Neither car fared particularly well in competition, posting thirds and fourths in class, until 004 received a revised twin-inlet Rochester fuel-injection system. Fitted with this, Thompson won outright at Watkins Glen in August but that was it for the season: sundry breakages sidelining both cars in the remaining races.

Dick Thompson was bitterly disappointed that Chevrolet did not back the Grand Sport Corvette. He raced a 1963 Corvette, again fitted with the new ZO6 road race option package for the Gulf Oil Company, but the new Cobra outclassed it.

Remembering the Grand Sport years later, Thompson recounted: "The first engine in the lightweight was really something. It was an all-aluminum 377 cubic inch job, fitted with Weber carburetors, and when I drove that thing in Nassau for Grady, it really flew!"

"I also drove a Grand Sport with Dick Gulstrand for the Penske team at Sebring in 1966. The car I drove for Roger had a Traco-built 427 in it and, at 1800 pounds, it moved. God only knows how much horsepower that thing had. That was perhaps the fastest car I ever drove and was certainly the fastest car at Sebring that year."

"Those lightweights had tremendous potential but of course GM wouldn't provide any help or let any of the needed parts out for Grady or anyone else."

"I remember Roger Penske saying: 'They have those 377s sitting up there that are 100 pounds lighter than what I'm using and they put out just as much horsepower and I can't touch them!' It was very frustrating for all of us."

Both 003 and 004 went back to Chevrolet after the season and were fitted, along with 005, with the 377 cubic inch aluminum engine, this time with single sparkplug per cylinder. These engines were rated at 485bhp at 6000rpm and required a new hood to fit atop the four huge 58mm Weber carburetors, which replaced the fuel injection set up. Duntov entrusted

In March 1975, vintage racer Kent Painter bought the old 1964 Corvette that Dick Gulstrand had used to such effect. This is a photo of the car as Kent collected it. [Photo: Courtesy of Kent Painter.]

these three Grand Sports to John Mecom's racing team. Mecom, the son of a Houston oil millionaire, had hired the best of talent for his team. For drivers, he had Roger Penske, Augie Pabst, Jim Hall, Dick Thompson and A. J. Foyt.

The Mecom Racing Team was entered in the Nassau Speed Weeks held in December, and Chevrolet engineers accompanied the team to lend a helping hand. Three races were entered, the Tourist Trophy, the Governor's Cup and the Nassau Trophy. In the Tourist Trophy, two cars driven by Hall and Thompson both retired with differential failures. In the following week, the engineers worked to fix the problem by adding oil coolers to the top of the rear bodywork.

In the Governor's Cup, all three Grand Sports finished in the top six, comprehensively beating out their Shelby Cobra rivals. In the Nassau Trophy race, despite pitting to have their hoods taped down, Dick Thompson and John Cannon finished in fourth and eighth places respectively. Again, they had beaten the Cobras. The Grand Sports were eleven seconds a lap faster than the Cobras!

On the Monday following this race, John Mecom allowed the respected motoring Journalist Bernard Cahier to drive one of the Grand Sports and Cahier, like everyone who drove a Grand Sport, was amazed by the acceleration, reporting that he could spin the wheels in any gear. Cahier also noted that, at speed on the straight, the Grand Sport became light at the front and the steering felt very light.

Upon returning to Detroit, Duntov again had Chevrolet management on his back for breaking the "no-race" agreement with the other major American manufacturers, and the Grand Sport project was shelved yet again. Duntov side-stepped the agreement this time by giving the cars out to private racers such as Grady Davis. Delmo Johnson, a Chevrolet dealer, bought Davis' car for some $8,000. Two other cars escaped the Chevrolet factory: 005 went to Jim Hall who sent it to Roger Penske's shop for preparation for the Sebring 12-Hour race, and 003 once more went back to John Mecom for preparation for Sebring.

For nine hours, Foyt and John Cannon ran in the top ten but then lost a wheel and Penske, having led the first lap, broke a half-shaft. That was replaced by one "borrowed" from a spectator's Corvette! Both cars finished the race, but were well down the field, although Roger Penske did post one lap just a second short of John Surtees' winning Ferrari 250P. After this, there was little action on the Grand Sport front until Road America in September, where 005 was driven by Roger Penske, Hall and Hap Sharp. Penske dueled furiously with Ken Miles in his Cobra until having to concede the place towards the end of the race.

In September, the Bridgehampton Double 500 scored points towards the International Manufacturers' Championship and Frank Dominiani took his Corvette to finish fourteenth, just two places ahead of another Corvette, this one driven by Skip Sofield and Tom McNeil, which was the last finisher. Dominiani finished twelfth in the next year's race.

In October, Penske loaned 005 to Ben Moore to run in a Regional race at Reading, Pennsylvania, where Moore romped home an easy winner and then Mecom prepared his car for Nassau by stripping three hundred pounds of weight from it. John Mecom sent his car, to be driven by Jack Saunders. The big surprise was that Carroll Shelby brought the prototype of the 427 cubic inch Cobra to the meeting but Penske beat Miles in a 5-lap race on the morning of the Nassau Trophy. In the big race itself, Miles built an early lead but Penske gradually reeled him in until the Cobra's engine failed, leaving the victory in a rain-shortened race to Roger Penske. Jack Saunders acquitted himself well until retiring on the eighteenth lap. After the race, 005 was sold by Penske to George Wintersteen.

The Grand Sports raced once again at Sebring, in 1965. Wintersteen's 005 finished fourteenth overall in the year of the great flood and Delmo Johnson prepared 003 with a "special" 454 cubic inch engine. That car finished in thirty-sixth place.

At the beginning of 1966, Roger Penske bought the last remaining Grand Sports, 001 and 002, and sold 002 to George Wintersteen. It was at this point that Dick Gulstrand arrived on the Grand Sport scene. Gulstrand had won three consecutive SCCA Championships in C-Production Sting Rays, beating the Cobras. Penske hired Gulstrand to race prepare 001 with a "special" aluminum-headed 427 "mystery" motor and de-tuned it (in the interests of reliability) to 500bhp. For Sebring, Gulstrand shared the roadster with Dick Thompson, whilst the production coupe was driven by Wintersteen and Ben Moore. In the race, Thompson was forced off course by an errant Morgan and bent the chassis and punctured the sump. End of race for the Grand Sport.

George Wintersteen raced his Grand Sport in the USRRC series right through until June 1966 when he sold it. Despite its age, the Grand Sport put in a good account of itself.

Chapter Three

MAINLY BIG BLOCKS
1965 to 1983

Orlando Costanzo in his big block 427 Corvette that he shared with Dave Heinz of Tampa, Florida. It is seen here at Sebring in 1971. [Photo: Courtesy of Orlando Costanzo.]

Despite the Shelby Cobra stamping over just about everything in its class (in particular SCCA A-Production), private Corvette owners did have some good struggles with them. In 1965, John Martin from Missouri managed to win his class in the Midwest division. George Robertson, Jr. and Dick Boo won the Sebring 12-Hours (in their class). Corvettes would go on to win the Sebring class right up until 1972, when the class structure was changed as the FIA mandated a GT era of racing, which produced such hybrids as the Porsche RSR and 935.

Upping the Ante – 1965 to 1967

For 1965, Chevrolet, in response to the domination of both national and international competition by the AC Cobra, introduced the big block engine into the production car line up.

1966 saw the introduction of the classic 427 cubic inch big block and with this 0–60mph came up in a shattering 4.8 seconds and 0–100mph in 11.2 seconds, all this in a car that would achieve 140mph flat out.

In 1967, Jerry Thompson and Tony de Lorenzo got together to form the Owens-Corning Racing Team. Owens-Corning made the fiberglass that went into the fabrication of the Corvette's bodies and provided sponsorship for the team.

Jerry Thompson: "I met Tony in 1967 and we each bought an L88 Stingray roadster and shared the driving. In 1968, Tony built a new Corvette racer out of a car that his father, a GM executive, got out of the executive car park. We did the Daytona 24-Hours in this car and I can remember getting on the brakes but the relay rod on the steering folded over to give toe-out on the steering. On top of that, an outer wheel bearing burned out on the banking."

"When we got back to Chevrolet and told Zora (Arkus-Duntov), he immediately had the bearing size changed and welded a strengthening bar into the relay rod. I guess you could say that racing does improve the breed."

"We ran the rest of that 1968 season in SCCA races in Tony's parts car with a 327 engine but the Cobras had won since they were introduced and we had to settle for second overall at the run-offs."

Orlando Costanzo had the very first 396 cubic inches big block off the production line and immediately took it racing. "I would do about twelve races a year. Our Corvettes had the Confederate flag painted on them to make them stand out amongst the other cars."

"Zora (*Arkus-Duntov–Author*) would make sure I got all the right parts to go race with. He'd call me the week before every race, asking: 'You are gonna be there, aren't you?'"

Orlando Costanzo entered his big-block 427 Corvette in the Sebring 12-Hours of 1967. His co-drivers were Gene Guy and Dave McLain. In this photograph, taken shortly before the start, he is seen standing on the right of the car with a Chevrolet engineer standing on the left. {Photo: Courtesy of Orlando Costanzo.]

In this next photograph, Orlando Costanzo is running towards his big-block Corvette at the start of the 1967 Sebring 12-Hour race. [Photo: Courtesy of Orlando Costanzo.]

"The big-block Corvettes handled real well. 'Course, they were heavy but man, they were fast. I made money when I sold the 1965 car and I bought a 1966 'Vette with the 427 engine making 650 horsepower. I told the kid that I sold it to afterwards: 'Listen, you look after it and this engine'll go forever.' He went and did drag races and was never beaten in the year afterwards."

Depression shows on the face of the corner worker guarding Orlando Costanzo's Corvette after it was put out of the 1967 Sebring 12-Hour race in an accident. [Photo: Courtesy of Orlando Costanzo.]

"Those big block 'Vettes had so much power and torque, they'd tear up rear ends and gearboxes if you didn't drive them with that in mind. Zora told me that engine was safe to 7,500rpm but I never shifted above 6,500. There wasn't any need. Any broken parts got sent back to Chevrolet where the engineers analyzed the problem and made new, stronger parts. That's what you call development."

Bill Tower, who today owns the 1956 Betty Skelton record-breaking Corvette, and the number 005 Grand Sport coupe, graduated from the GN Institute in 1966 and went straight to work at the GM Technical Center. "I was set straight to work helping Jim Hall with aluminum big block engines for his Chaparral project. They were very well engineered cars. We concentrated on putting reliability into his engines, because he could take all the power that we could supply and drive the car (and engine!) to its limits."

Walt Lister's 396 Corvette, pictured here at Autocross events in 1966. [Photo: Courtesy of Walt Lister.]

"Then I concentrated on the L88 road cars. They went to the very elite, such as Douane, Rathmann and Yenko. Chevrolet had a lot of problems with the 427 early on. They were really let out too early. No-one at the dealers had any school time on them and they broke rodbolts, valve springs and generally overheated. We concentrated on each part until the problems were solved and then the big blocks were very reliable, finishing almost every race."

At Le Mans in 1967, Bob Bondurant shared this 427 'Vette with Dick Gulstrand. They were put out when leading their class, by engine failure during the night. In front of the Corvette is the Le Mans course car, a Ferrari 330 GT. [Photo: Courtesy of The Klemantaski Collection.]

Dick Gulstrand with Mark Marabella in 2001. Mark bought the ex-Walt Lister 396 Corvette that Dick maintained in the sixties and seventies and still owns it today. [Photo: Courtesy of Mark Marabella.]

The new big block Corvette was so tractable, it could also be used for autocross events and this was a route taken by Dennis McCosh in California: "I had started racing in 1959 in Austin-Healeys and MGs. A pal bought a 1965 396 Corvette in 1967 and we started racing it in High Speed Solo 1 and 2. I bought the car in 1969. We fitted the Gulstrand rear suspension links which helped keep the rear wheels more upright in hard cornering and were very successful with the car right up to the early '70s."

"We replaced the 396 with a 427 cubic inch short block somewhere around 1970 but the bottom end let go at a meeting in Santa Maria. We pulled the 427 out, sleeved two cracked cylinders in the old 396 and stuck that back in, together with an enlarged oil pan. The car ran just fine and I kept her until 1998, when I decided a friend was better off with her than me leaving her to stand in the garage."

Walt Lister was another Californian who had autocrossed a 396 Corvette and remembered it with fondness: "I had started racing with a Jaguar XK120M and then bought an Austin-Healey. In 1965, I bought a 396 'Vette from Dick Gulstrand. It was just four months old and had 11,000 miles on it. It came with the close ratio gearbox, 4/11 gears and solid lifters. I ran it on Stock Car Special tires that were as hard as rocks and they would

Walt Lister's 396 Corvette, driven by a friend at the Bob Bondurant Race School. The Friend? Elliott Forbes-Robinson. [Photo: Courtesy of Walt Lister.]

last a season. At that time, Autocross was big in Southern California, there were two or three events every weekend. You could get up to four hundred entries for any single event. There were at least thirty to forty 'Vettes in there. You had to be good to make it into the top ten."

For 1966, Duntov introduced, as we have seen, the 427 cubic inch engine and this, in L88, 560bhp tune, plus the F-41 specification heavy duty suspension, brakes and Positraction rear axle, looked as if it might beat the Cobra. Unfortunately, the Cobras were still a third lighter than the L88 and the Cobras had almost as much power.

Corvette

Long Distance Warriors – Corvettes at Le Mans, Daytona and Sebring

The Big Block, 427 cubic inch engined Corvette was homologated by the FIA in October 1965. In the homologation sheet, the car is described as a "Corvette 19437 Coupe" and the form went on to state that five hundred of these Corvettes had been built between September 7th and 28th. The engine's bore and stroke was 4.25 by 3.76 inches. Wheelbase was given as 98.0 inches. Front track was 58.9 inches and rear track was 59.7 inches (with the optional seven inch wide wheels). Fuel capacity was 36.5 U.S. gallons and the weight of the car, with water, oil and spare wheel but without fuel and tools was 2900 pounds.

Walt Lister competing at an Autocross in California in the late sixties. Walt was very successful in this type of competition with his Dick Gulstrand-modified 396 Corvette. [Photo: Courtesy of Walt Lister.]

The First Four Decades of Racing Success

Chevrolet's two main contenders competed many times at Daytona. Here is a Camaro passing a big block Corvette on the banking some time in the late '60s. [Photo: Courtesy of Orlando Costanzo.]

Bob Johnson in later years. This photo was taken in 1972 when he and Dave Heinz shared this open Corvette to place fourth in the "Presidential 250" race at Daytona on November 19th. [Photo: Courtesy of NASCAR/IMSA Collection.]

Where International competition was concerned (particularly in the long-distance races), it was a different story. Roger Penske, Dick Gulstrand, Ben Moore and George Wintersteen teamed together in the Daytona Continental and finished first in the GT class, twelfth overall: At Sebring they won their class again, this time finishing ninth overall.

Dick Gulstrand: "I was Roger Penske's first hired driver. I was also sponsored by a Chevrolet dealer, Hi Baher, who wanted to sell more Corvettes from his dealership. We got sponsorship from Sunoco, Sunray Oil, GTX and other oil companies. That big block Corvette really handled well once you learned how to set it up. It was difficult to keep the nose down but that was the trick to making them go fast. I guess we were doing 180-190 mph at Daytona when we won the 24-Hours. On skinny tires too!"

"After winning at Sebring, we went to Le Mans. What a blast. We led everyone for hours until the engine let go. You can't imagine how distraught I was when that happened. To have won Daytona, Sebring and Le Mans in one year would have been a terrific achievement for us."

John Greenwood and Dick Smothers at Sebring in 1971 during the 12-Hour race. They won the GT class outright, placing seventh overall. [Photo: Courtesy of Jack Boxstrom Collection.]

John Greenwood celebrates his victory after winning at Watkins Glen in July 1971.
[Photo: Courtesy of Jack Boxstrom Collection.]

The next year, 1967, Don Yenko and Dave Morgan won the GT class at Sebring. Sadly, neither of James Garner's two Corvettes featured in the results. One car, driven by Dick Gulstrand, Ed Leslie, Scooter Patrick and Dave Jordan was not classified owing to not covering enough laps, and the other car, crewed by Scooter Patrick, Dave Jordan and Herb Caplan, had its engine fail after 262 laps. Dick Gulstrand and Bob Bondurant teamed up with a big block Corvette at the Le Mans 24-Hours and were leading the class by miles in the smart red, white and blue coupe, when the engine failed in the thirteenth hour.

After his first 1964 race Corvette, Tony de Lorenzo raced, of all things, a Chevrolet Corvair in 1965 and 1966 before buying another Corvette to race. "That Corvair taught me a lot about car control and momentum! For 1967, I received sponsorship from the local Chevrolet dealer, Henley Dawson. He ordered an L-88 and I went off to do SCCA National races. I remember that we won the first race at Road America, Elkhart Lake. Then we got into breaking transmissions and rear ends. I went to the run-offs at Daytona and finished second."

The wonderful Scuderia Filipinetti-entered big block Corvette of Henry Greder and Reine Wisell. The gearbox couldn't take the strain and cried "enough" after 196 laps at Le Mans in 1969. It is seen here receiving attention in the pits. [Photo: Courtesy of The Klemantaski Collection.]

Jerry Thompson, Tony's partner in the Owens-Corning team remembered: "1969, I crashed out of the Daytona 24-Hours but we won at Sebring. In the national races, we at last beat the Cobras, finishing first and second in SCCA. We got a lot of press out of that."

"We had some interesting experiences with Corvette racing. In 1969, Tony and I were leading our class at Daytona. Going into the darkness, I was up on the banking when the engine just shut off. I coasted into the pits and told the chief mechanic that I thought the rotor arm in the distributor had broken. He dived under the hood and replaced it. Sure enough, the engine fired right up and I pulled back out of the pits. I had just got into no mans land when the propshaft fell off due to a broken U-joint. Of course, the vibration from the failing joint had shaken the rotor arm loose. As I lay there in the darkness underneath the car, getting burnt and covered in grease as I changed the joint, I couldn't help thinking that I could have been more thoughtful!"

Technically, the Corvettes built for the Owens-Corning team used the L-88 engine of 427 cubic inches, giving 600 horsepower from 6500 to 7000rpm. These engines went into L-88 chassis, equipped with J-56 disc brakes, which used semi-metallic brake pads and

Two of the main protagonists of 1971 in the IMSA GT Championship are seen here: Bill Schumacher of Detroit is leading Dave Heinz of Tampa, Florida. Both are in "big block" Corvettes. [Photo: Courtesy of IMSA Collection.]

a special proportioning valve for front to rear braking effort. Springing on the suspension was stiffened, along with a thicket anti-rollbar. K-66 fully transistorized ignition was fitted, as was an M-22 "Rock crusher" gearbox, and an M-80 rear end fitted with 'Positraction' (limited slip differential). The engine and transmission were blueprinted and the chassis beefed up with strengthening brackets. Fuel tank capacity was 42 gallons and Heim joints were used in place of the standard rubber fittings.

Bob Johnson still lives in Ohio and he recounted how he got involved with racing Corvettes: "My business partner bought one of the first Triumph TR4s in the State. He encouraged me to go along to a road race and I caught the bug. Next thing was, I knew a kid

Daytona 1972: As you can see by the "Camel" sticker behind the driver's door of this "big block" Corvette, sponsorship had arrived in GT racing in America. [Photo: Courtesy of NASCAR/IMSA Collection.]

who had a race-prepped Spitfire and I asked him: 'Lend me your car, I'll give you two new tires and I'll do driver's school. If I damage the car, I'll pay for it.' I did the school and was voted the 'most outstanding driver.' I entered my first sportscar race in the Spitfire at the old Canalsville airport and won. Now I was really hooked!"

"For 1967, another friend lent me his 1966 street coupe and I entered the 'A' Production SCCA race at Cumberland and won that. I qualified third in the Mid-West region that year and so I got to go to the run-offs at Daytona. I qualified fourth and, in the race, worked my way up to second before a head gasket let go and I had to settle for fifth place."

Henry Greder bought his big block Corvette from the Scuderia Filipinetti and carried on campaigning it at Le Mans. In 1970, Greder and Jean Paul Rouget finished a resounding sixth overall and won the GT class outright. [Photo: Courtesy of The Klemantaski Collection.]

Corvettes were raced around the World. Curt Wetzel raced this big block Sting Ray at the Avus-Rennen on, appropriately enough, the fourth of July, 1971. [Photo: Author's Collection.]

For 1968, the Corvette appeared with a new, more slippery body, the roadster version with its hardtop affixed proving to be more aerodynamically efficient than its coupe brother.
The designer of this body shape was David Holls and the design was based upon the Mako Shark II that had been appearing at various auto shows during the previous year.

Strangely, although it looked more aerodynamic than the previous 1963 to 1967 design, wind tunnel tests proved that it was not as efficient, thus putting back the car's introduction until 1968. The car's introduction had originally been planned for 1967.

In terms of numbers sold, this new 1968 Corvette broke all previous records. 28,566 were sold but this was beaten handsomely by the 1969 model, which sold 38,762.

From 1970 to 1972, the body shape remained very much the same as the earlier cars but 1970 saw the end of the 427 engine. Increasing emission laws meant that the big block

Above and facing page: John Greenwood's Corvette at Le Mans in 1973, prior to the start of the race. [Photos: Courtesy of Jack Boxstrom Collection.].

engine was coming to the end of its life in the Corvette. One more large engine appeared, the 454 cubic inch model, in 1971. This had been designed to run on lower octane fuel, and was quoted as delivering 465 horsepower at 5,600rpm.

Jerry Grant and Dave Morgan entered one of the 1968 Corvettes in the Daytona Continental and won the class, coming in tenth overall. At Sebring, Morgan teamed with Hap Sharp and they won the class there, too. James Garner's American International racing Corvettes also did well there.

Tony de Lorenzo again: "For 1968, I joined the Sunray DX team with Jerry Thompson, Peter Revson, Don Yenko, Jerry Grant and Dave Morgan. We ran a Corvette at Daytona that was built-up by Gib Hofstetter, a chassis engineer with Chevrolet. Hofstetter really went to town on that car. He had new front hubs, spindles, bigger half-shafts made. In fact, he went right through the transmission of the car, improving it everywhere. We had no problems with it at all. Jerry Grant and Dave Morgan won the class, finishing tenth and Peter Revson and Don Yenko finished fourth in class. Jerry Thompson and I didn't cover enough distance to be classified as finishers, but we were still fifth in class. At Sebring, we broke a driveshaft after just forty-eight laps and were out."

In 1969, an aluminum block was available under the title "ZL-1." This block weighed forty pounds less than a steel 327 block. Corvettes were getting much faster on the race track.

Two big block Corvettes were entered at Le Mans in 1968. These were the Scuderia Filipinetti cars driven by Sylvain Garant and Jean-Michel Giorgi, with Henri Greder and Umberto Maglioli, the great Italian long-distance racer. They were to become a big favorite with the crowd at Le Mans and participate for a remarkable number of years. This year saw one have an engine let go and the other crash. The two Robert Johnsons crewed a Corvette for the Watkins Glen 6-Hours in July. One Johnson was distinguished by having "R." as a middle name. Whatever, the Johnsons won the GT class, placing eleventh overall.

Bob Johnson: "Well, in 1968, my friend, whose Corvette I had been racing, bought a 427 'big-block' 'Vette. With my namesake, another Bob Johnson, we won the GT class in the Watkins Glen 6-Hours. I still have the lap record, as they changed the track afterwards."

1969 also saw the incorporation of IMSA, the new sanctioning body whose encouragement was to take the big block Corvettes to a new level of power and performance. In that year, the A-Production Championship was won by Jerry Thompson, whilst B-Production went to Allan Barker in a 327-engined version. At Daytona, for the twenty-four hour race, Smokey Drolet, John Tremblay and Vince Gimondo won the GT class. Next year, 1970, Jerry Thompson and Dave Mahler won the GT class at the Daytona 24-Hours in a Corvette entered by Tony de Lorenzo, placing as high as sixth overall. At Sebring, Tony shared his car with Dick Lang to win the GT class for Corvette yet again.

It was around this time that Mike Brockman started racing Corvettes: "The first one that I raced was Bruce Baron's 1968 candy apple red and metalflake gold car. It had a 350 small block in it and it had belonged to Vince Gimondo. I bought it off of his wife. I did SCCA races in Florida and once traveled as far as Savannah, Georgia. That was a good car and gave me a good grounding in how they handled."

At Le Mans this year, the Scuderia Filipinetti-entered car of Henri Greder and Reine Wisell retired when the gearbox failed at two-thirds distance. 1970 saw a Corvette finish well up, although only seven cars were classified as finishers, having covered sufficient distance to be classified. Just behind the seventh car, a Porsche 911S, was Henri Greder, this time in his own car, partnered by Jean-Pierre Rouget. Another French-entered big block Corvette was that of Ecurie Leopard but it was forced out in an accident at the five-hour mark. This car

In 1970, Duntov drew another mid-engined GM race car. This was Cerv-II, seen here in testing. Like Cerv-I, it never raced. [Photo: Used with permission of GM Media Archives.]

By 1972, Henry Greder's big block 'Vette was becoming somewhat long in the tooth but Greder tried again at Le Mans; this time he was accompanied by Marie-Claude Charmasson. Sadly, after 235 laps, she was involved in an accident with the second placed Matra and put out. In 1973, the pairing came back to win the GT class yet again. This 1969 Corvette appeared twice more at Le Mans in 1974 and 1975, having entered and run at Le Mans no less than seven times. [Photo: Courtesy of The Klemantaski Collection.]

John Greenwood's big-block Corvette in victory circle at Daytona in 1974. [Photo: Courtesy of Steve Golden.]

Left: John Greenwood was a great champion of the Corvette but rarely got the better of: "Them damn furrin cars." Still, his Corvettes were some of the most dramatic cars to be seen on any racetrack. This is Greenwood's "Spirit of America" 'Vette of 1974 photographed at Charlotte. [Photo: Courtesy of Motor Racing Graphics/IMSA Collection.]

Below: The cockpit of John Greenwood's wide-bodied Corvette "Spirit of Le Mans 76." [Photo: Courtesy of Steve Golden.]

was back at Le Mans the following year, but the transmission failed at sixteen hours. Henri Greder's car blew its engine just one hour earlier.

"Doug Bergen bought a 1969 big block Corvette," remembers Bob Johnson. "He got us to drive it and we were lying first in GT in the Daytona 24-Hours when a drive-shaft failed

John Greenwood's #48 Corvette at Daytona. [Photo: Courtesy of the Jack Boxstrom Collection.]

with just thirty minutes to go. Nevertheless, we did finish second in the GT class at Sebring that year. For 1970, I partnered John Greenwood at Michigan. He was using BF Goodrich street radial tires but we managed to win."

Someone else who encountered John Greenwood in 1970 was Jerry Thompson. "I was the chief instructor at the driving school that John came to. I'm sure that his ambition was to beat both Tony and I. I remember that Tony, John and I went to the run-offs that year and the competition was intense between us."

"I remember driving with John once, in one of his 'wide-body' Corvettes. That was a killer car, huge cross-ram injection. I started the race and we had the race won, beating Hobbs and Posey in their BMW. Then John took over. He only had to maintain the lead, but he drove every lap as if he were qualifying for pole. 'Course, half an hour of that and the M22 tranny was melted."

John Greenwood in his #49 Corvette at Sebring in 1971. [Photo: Courtesy of the Jack Boxstrom Collection.]

John Greenwood buckling himself into one of his early Corvettes in 1970. [Photo: Courtesy of the Jack Boxstrom Collection.]

A 454 cubic inch engine could now be ordered (the LS-5) and the suspension specification was now called the ZR-2 option. Allan Barker won the SCCA B-Production Championship for four straight years in his Corvette, 1969-1972. He then sold the Corvette to Bill Jobe, who won the Championship in 1973 and 1974.

One of the few in racing who bucked the trend to race a big block, was "Fast" Phil Curran. "I did my first SCCA drivers' school in 1969 at Nelson Ledges with my 1963 split-window Corvette. I had bought this car from the local Pontiac dealership. They'd taken it in on a trade-in and it didn't run worth a damn. It was a 'Fuelie' (*Rochester mechanical*

John Greenwood winning the 1974 Daytona Finale in one of his own Corvettes. Ironically, although John Greenwood's Corvettes were faster than the Porsche opposition, the Carreras nearly always came out on top due to faster, more co-ordinated fuel stops. Additionally, fuel consumption in the smaller-engined Carreras was much lower than in the big block Corvettes. [Photo: Courtesy of IMSA Collection.]

John Greenwood with his Corvette in 1970 at Road America, Elkhart Lake.
[Photo: Courtesy of the Jack Boxstrom Collection.]

fuel injection–Author) and no-one knew how to fix it. I bought a manual and studied the injection's layout. When I looked the set-up over, I discovered that it was just one screw that needed adjusting to make it run right!"

"I was in college in Florida at the time, just a student, and I saw that there was a local autocross being held nearby, so I entered it. I won first time out. I still have the sterling silver trophy that I won and I treasure it. I had a Chevrolet Impala as a company car then and I welded on a towing hitch myself and I flat towed my now-racecar, complete with race tires inside, to Nelson Ledges and Watkins Glen to race in the SCCA regional races. At Watkins, over the three races, I placed first, second and third."

"To show you what SCCA racing was like back then, one of the other Corvette competitors noticed that I had filed the fiberglass right back over the wheel wells in order to get the widest tires in there that I could. This guy came up to me and said: 'I can protest you

The also-rans. Although they tried hard, neither Chevrolet, with their Corvettes and Camaros, nor BMW, could beat the Porsche Carreras on a regular basis in the IMSA Camel GT Championship. In 1974, on June 30th, 41,000 spectators watched this duel between the BMW CSL of Brett Lunger/George Follmer and John Buffum and the Corvette of Jerry Thompson and Don Yenko at the five-hour race held at Mid-Ohio. They finished fifth and sixth respectively. [Photo: Courtesy of Motor Racing Graphics/IMSA Collection.]

for that.' Luckily, he didn't. Shortly after this, in 1970, in fact, I was drafted into the army for Vietnam and sent to Augusta, Georgia. I asked the C.O. if he minded my going racing and he didn't like the idea, so I used an assumed name to race under."

"By now I had my SCCA National license and I won the SCCA race at Road Atlanta. The month before this, I had crashed the car at Talladega in the Charlie Kemp memorial race on the Sunday. The day before, I had run my last regional race there and got my National license. I hit the wall and the 'Vette flipped over onto its roof. I had to hire a wrecking truck to get me back home. It cost me $270 to straighten the chassis but I got it all back together

Success! John Greenwood led the last lap of the 1975 IMSA Daytona Finale, the only other driver on the same lap being Brian Redman in his BMW CSL. Greenwood ran out the winner by forty seconds. [Photo: Courtesy of IMSA Collection.]

with the help of duct tape and off we went to Road Atlanta. I remember I blew the engine in the third race, but still managed to finish well."

In 1971, Tony de Lorenzo and John Mahler, partnered by Don Yenko, won the GT class in the Daytona 24-Hours, finishing fourth overall. At Sebring, John Greenwood has his first taste of International success, winning the GT class in conjunction with Dick Smothers.

By 1976, John Greenwood's Corvettes had become, if possible(!), even more voluptuous. 1976 saw his car racing at Daytona and Le Mans in the 24-Hour race. [Photo: Courtesy of IMSA Collection.]

Rick Mancuso's Greenwood-built big-block Corvette at Sebring in 1976. Just look at that Kinsler injection set-up! [Photo: Courtesy of Steve Golden.]

John Greenwood, partnered by Robert R. Johnson, also won their class in the Watkins Glen 6-Hours, placing fifth overall.

In this year, the first IMSA races for what would later become the Camel GT Championship were being run. Dave Heinz from Tampa, Florida, teamed with Orlando

Costanzo and Don Yenko to win three races outright, including the inaugural IMSA Camel GT race at the Virginia International Raceway in Danville. Dave Heinz, with five class wins in his big block Corvette, took the Grand Touring over 2.5 liter class (GTO).

Orlando Costanzo: "I last competed at Talladega in 1971 and that was about my best race. There were many big cars in that race. Right there, I decided that the investment needed to keep Corvettes winning was going to be too much, so I retired."

Someone else who would race in IMSA for years to come in Corvettes was Phil Currin: "I was going to race at Road Atlanta at the end of 1971 in the 'B' Production division run-offs. Someone said: 'There's a race on Saturday at Daytona,' but I knew I had to be careful to preserve my car for the run-offs. Nevertheless, we heard that this new IMSA organization paid money to racers and sure enough, at this Daytona Finale, I won $250. Then I went to the run-offs and finished sixth."

"Most of the other guys were using big blocks but I tried a 427 cubic inch once, bent the valves the first time that I missed a shift, and went back home. I pulled the heads and studied the combustion chambers (I did all my own engine work). Right away, I saw that there was only 20 thou. of an inch clearance between the pistons and valves. You need at least a hundred and twenty thou. I put my old small-block engine back in and went just as fast. The small-block engine suited my style of driving, I could throw the car around a lot. You couldn't do that with the big block cars. They were for going fast down the straights. Trouble was, the power overloaded all the transmission and rear end and caused a lot of reliability problems that I didn't have."

The first IMSA yearbook reported: *"Thundering Corvettes that owned GTO."*

Bob Johnson remembered 1971 well. "I got into a deal with Don Yenko to run a Chevrolet Vega to race. We took it to Daytona and I blew three engines in three days, trying to qualify that car. We were sharing a pit garage with Or Costanzo and he invited me to co-drive with him. We finished second both there and at Sebring."

In 1972, Camel Cigarettes sponsored the IMSA series, making it "The Camel GT Challenge Series" and, although Corvettes did well, winning outright at Daytona (Charlie Kemp and Wilbur Pickett), Donnybrooke (Denny Long) and Talladega (Wilbur Pickett), it was the Porsche 911 of Hurley Haywood that won the overall Championship.

Phil Currin won the GTO class in a 327 Corvette but did not score as many points as Haywood to take the overall Championship. Nevertheless, it was a creditable effort, considering that Phil's car was the oldest in the series as it was a 1963 model. His pit crew consisted of his wife, Ginny, and his brother, Tiger.

Phil: "I had been doing a support race to the Daytona Continental the day before, the 6-Hour race. In that race, I dropped out when a fuel injector broke. Upon impulse, I said to the crew: 'Let's do the Six-Hours!' My race number was 99 and it transpired that there had been

The Garcia Brothers and crew proudly wheel their Greenwood-style big-block Corvette to the start of the Sebring 12-Hour race in 1976. [Photo: Courtesy of Steve Golden.]

a Ferrari entered under that number but he never appeared and so I started in the Corvette instead of him. We found a co-driver, Bob Whitaker and I drove for five hours, my co-driver for one! Towards the end, I lost a seal in a caliper and all the fluid leaked out, so that I had no brakes at all. As there was just thirty minutes to go, I decided to try and finish with no brakes. I went out and Andretti passed me going into the horseshoe in his Ferrari 312P. He ducked in front of me and braked hard. I nearly hit him! Luckily, I missed and we finished the race okay. Sadly, although we were twenty-first on the track, we weren't classified as we hadn't

The Garcia Brothers Corvette at Sebring in 1976. [Photo: Courtesy of Steve Golden.]

covered enough distance but the thing that annoyed me was that the newspaper showed the result as belonging to the Ferrari guy who was never there!"

Dave Heinz and Robert R. (Bob) Johnson won their class at Daytona and at Sebring, too. Bob: "Yeah, that rebel 'Vette that I shared with Dave was the best I ever drove. I remember that at Daytona, a Vice-President of Goodyear Tires came over to us and said: 'If you use our radial street tire, and win, we'll have your names out nationwide tomorrow.' He was as good as his word!"

And later... after a recovery truck had got it all wrong in pit lane. [Photo: Courtesy of Steve Golden.]

"That car handled real well. 'Course, we raced against Cobras that were a thousand pounds lighter than we were. We took a cooling fan from a Corvair and fixed one on either front wheel to draw the hot air out. With that fitted, we could out-brake Ferrari Daytonas and give the Cobras a hard time."

Corvettes went to Le Mans again this year, and Greenwood's two Corvettes qualified at a higher speed than any other GT car. Neither of these two big blocks lasted the distance, going out within an hour of one another with engine problems. It is probable that a lot of the Corvette engine problems at Le Mans were caused by the poor octane rating of the fuel supplied by the French race organizers, the Automobile Club de l'Ouest. The Ecurie Leopard engine was destroyed when only five hours from the finish, and the Greder-entered car was put out in an accident, less than three hours from the finish.

However, another big block Corvette did win its class at Le Mans this year, the Dave Heinz car that he shared with Robert Johnson, placing fifteenth overall. Bob: "Hmm, Le Mans. I still wake up in the middle of the night and remember that."

"I did 'B' Production in another Corvette and finished first in the central division. The National run-offs were at Road Atlanta that year and I qualified second and finished third – We had a Rochester carburetor and it kept cutting out over the hump on the main straight."

1973 saw far more professionalism come to IMSA. Porsche, in particular, backed

Phil Currin's Corvette before the start of the Daytona Finale in 1978. [Photo: Courtesy of Steve Golden.]

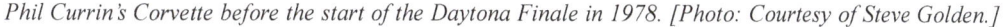

Right: March 19th, 1977 – John Carusso, Luis Sereix and Emory Donaldson, all from Florida, drove the number 48 big block Corvette in the Sebring 12 Hours. Sadly, they failed to finish, retiring on lap 59. [Photo: Courtesy of Steve Golden.]

Below: John Paul re-entered racing in 1978 with a Greenwood-style Corvette. Behind him in this photograph is Bill Whittington in his Porsche 935. Acting on the adage: "If you can't beat 'em, join 'em", Paul did exactly that and abandoned his Corvette in 1979 in favor of the first of four Porsche 935s that he and his son, John Paul, Jr., raced with success. [Photo: Courtesy of Bill Oursler.]

its drivers with a support truck and Peter Gregg, the eventual winner, certainly had what amounted to a "works" supported Carrera.

Despite the Porsche's winning combination of lightweight, power, handling and frugality where the gas consumption was concerned, Corvettes still did well. Ron Grable and Mike Brockman placed third overall at Daytona in the 24-Hours, the GT win being taken by the NART Ferrari Daytona of Francois Migault and Milt Minter. John Greenwood and Ron Grable took third overall in the Sebring 12-Hours but the GT win went to the first placed car, a Porsche Carrera RSR, driven by Peter Gregg, Hurley Haywood and Dave Helmick.

Tony de Lorenzo: "The best Corvette that I raced was undoubtedly the 1973 Budweiser sponsored car built by Mitch Markey. He teamed up with Lee Dykstra and they built a very special, stiffened chassis with brakes that really stopped the car well. Mitch tried all sorts

Whoever won the Indianapolis 500 race for single-seater race cars, won the pace car too. Just before the 1978 running of the race, the pace car is displayed on the track with Danny Ongais, of the Interscope team, in the center of the group. [Photo: GM 2001. Used with the permission of the GM Archives.]

Rich Dagiel, Joe Pirotta and Tom Nell ran this big block at Sebring in 1973. The car ran IMSA, Trans Am and SCCA races for many years. Joe Pirotta continues to race the car in vintage events today. [Photo: Courtesy of Ted Dagiel.]

of brakes – we had twin calipers, ali calipers – that car was really good in the long distance races. I guess that we should have spent more money on the engines, but that's another story. We were on pole for all the races we entered, the handling was that great."

Jerry Thompson: "I had raced a Corvette in 1972 that belonged to our chief engineer's son and it had a Reynolds aluminum block. At Daytona, Sam Posey was driving a Ferrari Daytona and protested us. Said it wasn't 'production spec.'"

"For 1973, I built a big block Corvette and Marshall Robins bought it. He had me drive it in the Trans Am where I found myself up against Milt Minter in a Porsche RSR. I usually ran out of brakes and used to finish third or fourth pretty regularly."

"For 1974, I built another big block, this time with boxed flares. At Mid-Ohio, I led every lap at a second under the lap record in the first hour, but eventually, Don Yenko and I had to settle for sixth place overall."

Phil Currin: "In 1973, I finished eleventh at the Sebring 12-Hour race with Dan Fortin and Bill Johnson. We'd used ordinary heavy-duty shock absorbers and they broke off at the rear by the eyelets that held them on. I'd never realized quite how bumpy Sebring was before that. In 1974, John Bishop strongly advised me to buy a new Corvette. Remember, I was still competing with my '63 split-window coupe."

"I found a kid with a trust-fund and he promptly bought John Greenwood's 427 'T' top 'Vette. This was the third of the 'Stars and Stripes' cars and it was the only original big block 'Vette that I raced. I remember that I hitched up the trailer and drove to Greenwood's place to pick it up. It was all-white and cost $16,000. I did just one race at Daytona in that car and beat all the other Corvettes. Right after the race, the new owner took the car off for himself, so it was back to the small block. The big advantage of that car was its fuel consumption of 6.5mpg. That way, I didn't need as many fuel stops as the big block cars. Later on, I drove Rick Hays' big block but I always preferred my small block car."

Dave Heinz finished on the same lap as Gregg at Daytona in April, while Corvettes finished in the top six in four more IMSA GT races. Dave's erstwhile driving partner, Bob Johnson, teamed up with John Greenwood but: "Daytona, Sebring, Watkins Glen, we never finished a race that year. John would always admonish me: 'Don't take the revs over 6800.' He would always take the first stint and the car never came in with less than 7200 on it!"

At last, Henri Greder's faith in his Corvette at Le Mans paid off; the car that he shared with Marie-Claude Beaumont came in twelfth place and won the big GT class. Even the Ecurie Leopard car finished, in eighteenth place overall and second in class. The next year, Greder's car won the class again. He had now competed with this car in no less than five Le Mans 24-Hour races! John Greenwood led the class but climbed out of his car after four hours, the engine dead.

Left: As late as 1980, this 1963 split-window Corvette was still racing in the endurance classic at Sebring. It was driven by Bard Boand, Robert Kivela and Raymond Irwin. They finished in fortieth place. [Photo: Courtesy of Steve Golden.]

The 70s were not kind to production cars, with the new emphasis on safety and the oil crisis. The Corvette was no exception. Whilst the body shape stayed more or less the same throughout this model's run (with a few minor styling touches), the engines became progressively less and less powerful as more and more smog equipment cluttered the engine bay. In fact, by 1975, power had sagged to just 165 net horsepower. That year also saw the last production roadster manufactured. From then on, Corvettes came with a "T" top in which the roof panels could only be removed for open air motoring. To boost sales Indy pace cars were produced with special paint jobs.

Wide Body Phenomenon – 1974 to 1983

The long-distance races at Daytona and Sebring were stricken from the calendar in 1974 due to the World oil shortage but, for Corvette fans, it was the start of a new era. John Greenwood had entered IMSA racing.

"My dad was a vice-president at General Motors so I got a lot of 'special' parts to play with. I started out street racing big block Chevrolets in Detroit when I was young. First of all, I had a Chevrolet Impala that I enlarged to 452 cubic inches and I raced every night on Woodward Avenue, seven nights a week. It would turn a 12.0 flat."

Joe Cotrone, Emory Donaldson and Phil Currin shared this Corvette at Sebring in 1980. [Photo: Courtesy of Steve Golden.]

"I used to come home from work and tune the engine before I went out to the streets. There was a C-type Jaguar with a Chrysler Hemi engine and a '57 Corvette with a big block motor. I could beat both to a hundred but after that … Then I got a '64 Corvette and I started with a 409, then a 452 cubic inch motor, with a roller camshaft. Then I started stomping on everyone. I was eighteen years old. I learned how to get traction from the start and how to get a power curve that worked."

"I built eighteen engines while I was living at home with my parents. After I had built three engines and had pulled them up from the basement, my parents allowed me to build them in the den. I had, by then, bought a 1968 'Vette, and built an L88 motor for it. That was a blueprinted 440 cubic inch job, and the car turned the quarter in 10.8 seconds. I was working as an instrument guy in a construction company, and made good money."

"My wife saw an autocross event in a parking lot and dared me to join in. I don't like to be embarrassed, so I joined in the next weekend. Remind yourself of all the development that I had carried out on my Corvette with suspension, brakes, all sorted and oil coolers on the transmission and rear end. I turned the first lap faster than everyone else and carried on raising the lap record. A lot of people brought their cars on trailers but I beat them all. When the event was over, I paid the organizers two dollars per lap and kept on going, improving my times."

David Horchler bought an ex-Greenwood big block, wide-bodied Corvette and campaigned it in the early '80s. He later sold the car to Bill Tower, who today also owns the 1956 Betty Skelton Corvette and one of the Grand Sport Corvettes of the '60s. [Photo: Courtesy of D. Horchler.]

"I went over to the Waterford Raceway and watched cars practicing. I thought: 'I can do that.' I joined the race school and they scared my attitude right out of me. I entered the next weekend's event and had ladies in SEATs *(Spanish-built Fiats–Author)*, beating me."

"I thought about this all over the winter. Then I went back to racing and beat the track record at Waterford, really learning how to set the car up. I won the SCCA Regional Championship. Then I won the 1969 Championship with a Camaro. I did the 1970 and '71 Daytona and Sebring events."

"In 1972 to 1973, I participated in a BF Goodrich program. 1972, with 60 series tires, we were quick. In 1973, with the aspect ratio reduced to 50 series only, we were two seconds slower than the year before."

"1974 was the start of our 'wide-body' Corvettes. I raced a black car with red and blue stripes. I did the Trans Am, doing just three races. I won two, and finished third in the Championship."

"Then came IMSA races. I had a good relationship with Sebring and started promoting the Twelve-Hour race there, with John Bishop's blessing. Actually, what happened was, in 1973 at Daytona, John spoke to Peter Gregg who came over and said: 'John wants me to promote the 12-Hour race, but I don't want to. Do you want to do it?' I said: 'I might.' So I started doing just that. In 1975, I also started promoting the Riverside 6-hour race."

"IMSA were real nice. I had a good relationship with them. The Ulmanns didn't want to keep going with Sebring and so I took it over till David Cowart and Charles Mendez took it over in 1978. At least, we kept the race going."

"Our Corvettes were designed to four-wheel drift. The tires lasted longer that way.

Typical engine of a Greenwood Corvette. This one is a 477 cubic inch displacement, with Donovan aluminum block, cross-ram Kinsler fuel injection and Brodix aluminum heads. [Photo: Author's Collection.]

They may have looked hairy to drive but were very safe. They were incredibly fast, I saw over 220 mph on the big straightaways and 206 on the bankings. Trouble was… I was so busy doing business, I was counting going racing as a hobby, to get away from it all! I was building my cars nonstop. Well, actually, the suspension parts, and I had too much to do."

"Why didn't our Corvettes win more often? You know, we were out there having a good time while people like Peter Gregg were out there with race strategies, meaning to win. Porsche 911s had the rearward weight distribution that enabled them to launch out of corners better than any front-engined car could."

"I was selling my Corvettes to anyone with the money. Most of them didn't have a race license. John Bishop once remarked: 'I'd appreciate it if you didn't sell these powerful cars to anyone who asked for one!' I remember one time, there was this doctor, he bought a Corvette from me in 1975. We went to Talladega and this guy led from the start. Then he had a slow spin and finished up in the infield. He got started again and after four or five laps, he was leading again! Then he spun again. Same place, same thing. He still overtook near everyone before the end. Great days."

Steve Golden of Miami bought the "Spirit of Le Mans" and the "Spirit of '76" cars later on and had them restored: "When I was a kid, I used to go watch Daytona and Sebring all the time. Nothing impressed me so much as when John Greenwood's cars started up. There was nothing like that sound."

Ron Grable: "I started racing in 1964, Dodge Formula A, then open wheel cars. By 1968, I was racing professionally in NASCAR. In 1973, I drove with John Greenwood at Daytona, Sebring and Le Mans. Those big blocks were great cars and I enjoyed them. They were handicapped by using BF Goodrich street tires. At Daytona to begin with, we could only do two laps on one set. That first year was dreadful. But, bit by bit, the tires and handling got better."

Mike Brockman again: "Ron Grable got me hooked up with John Greenwood's Corvettes. In 1973, Ron had been going to share one of John's Corvettes at Sebring but he and John had a falling out so John called me and asked me to drive with Ron. I hitch-hiked to Sebring where John had three Corvettes entered. The engines, I remember, were a 427, a 454 and a 501 cubic inch monster. All three 'Vettes were on BF Goodrich street tires as that was how John had done his sponsorship deal with them. I shared the 427 cubic inch engined car and we came in third overall. All the Chevrolet top brass were there, including Zora Arkus-Duntov, so it was pretty wonderful."

"John asked me to drive with him again in 1974 at Road Atlanta and it was in one of his 'Super 'Vettes.' It was fast as hell. Those cars were built by Bob Riley and he's a genius – he'd built the Indy Coyotes for Roger McCluskey and A. J. Foyt."

By 1980, the Corvette was struggling against the overwhelming success of the Porsche 935. Still, many of them soldiered on in the IMSA GTO class. Here is one entering the main straight at Sebring as the sun sets during the Twelve-Hour race. [Photo: Courtesy of Steve Golden.]

"John Greenwood is six feet six inches tall and I'm five foot nine inches. Somewhere, I have a photograph of me waiting to drive in the pits. I've got so much foam stuck to me, you can hardly tell who I am!"

"Next time I drove with John was at the 1976 Daytona 24-Hours. We were only on seven cylinders in qualifying but still wound up seventh on the grid. I took over the lead from Peter Gregg on the first lap and just ran away. That Super 'Vette would do 221mph on the banking and, without the chicane that's there now, you could dive into turn three flat out. I didn't believe it could be done but by lap three, I was doing it. The car would just kind of take a set and go straight through, no trouble. Bob Riley had engineered those cars so well, you could tell the difference in the handling if you put just a 1/8th inch Gurney flap on the rear wing. You could make those things dance, they were so adjustable."

"At Daytona, we led for thirteen hours, but they were the wrong thirteen! Bill King had built the engines and later, after he'd torn down the broken engine, we found that it had been detonating. Too much compression, I guess."

"Giant Jim Moore was my mechanic and a great guy. I remember that later in the season, I led at Pocono until something broke. I wanted to put a Hewland gearbox in the Corvette but the rules didn't allow it. At Ontario, Lee Gaug of Goodyear Tires came over and suggested that we should swap our seventeen inch wide rear tires for thirteen inch ones. We did and went even faster. Less frontal area on such a fast circuit."

Rick Mancuso is the son of a Chevrolet dealer and worked for his father from 1972 till 1979. Along the way, he started racing Corvettes. "I started with a 1958 'Vette in SCCA Mid-West competition. By 1973, I'd progressed to a 1965 Sting Ray and I did my first IMSA race in 1974. John Bishop (*President of IMSA–Author.*) told me: 'You shouldn't really be here as you don't have the right license but I'll let you start off the back of the grid. Keep out of trouble.' I did just that until Don Yenko came around to lap me. He gave me a tap on the rear that I had to catch. Afterwards, he came over to say hello. I said: 'Why'd you hit me like that?' He said: 'It's just my way of saying hello!' When it came to the pit allocations, I was pitted in the number one pit with John Greenwood and that's where we met. He was back from Le Mans then."

"In 1975, I bought a basically standard big block Corvette with a Greenwood wide-body conversion and, in 1976, I bought a new Greenwood Corvette. This got crashed in practice at Sebring and John fixed it, but then 'borrowed' it to do Road Atlanta as there was a problem with his own car. After that, he re-named it: 'Spirit of Le Mans,' and took it over to do the race. He had invited me to go as a co-driver but my father didn't like me racing and wouldn't give me time off from work! I did, however, get to do a commentary on the radio link, direct from Le Mans. It was a big thing in America, John Greenwood with a Corvette

As late as 1987, the Garcia-built big block, wide-bodied Corvette was still winning races. Here it is in Europe at Zolder. Coincidentally, another ex-Greenwood Corvette took second place in this race. [Photos: Courtesy of Heinz Roth.]

battling in France. After Le Mans, John gave me the car back and I did 1977 and 1978 at Daytona and Sebring with it."

"You know, that big block Corvette was one of the most exciting racecars I've ever driven. General Motors didn't really want to be out of racing at that time, although they told the World they were. I never had any bills from them. They gave me engines, transmissions, you name it. I paid for nothing."

"Those Greenwood Corvettes were fast. They were the epitome of everything a racing sportscar should be. By 1976, we were using 494 cubic inch engines bored out to 510 cubic inches. I remember John telling me at Sebring that year, as the mechanics were installing bolts to hold the tires on: 'When you come out of the hairpin in first gear, don't stand on it, the gear will break.' In practice, John had posted a lap time of 2.54. Peter Gregg, who was racing the works BMW CSLs and was a friend of John's, posted a 2.53 and came in all smiles. John went out and did a 2.52. They went back and fourth five or six times, until Gregg got down to a 2.50 dead. John then said: 'Watch this.' He climbed into his car and went out; 2.49 on the first lap. Then 2.48, then a 2.47. Gregg threw his helmet down the pit lane and stormed off. John came in and said: 'You know, it'll go faster if I want it to!'"

John Greenwood's 'Super Corvette' featured aluminum engines of 427, 454 and 467 cubic inches in ZL-1 form, whilst he used steel blocks up to 480 cubic inches. They

The Garcia Brothers' Corvette. [Photo: Courtesy of Steve Golden.]

had Chevrolet pistons and conrods in them, with Cane or Iskenderian rollers prodded by General Kinetics camshafts, that looked after the valve timing. The valve retainers were made by Greenwood, out of titanium. Clutches and flywheels were by Hurst-Schiefer and the dry-sump tank held twenty quarts of oil. Kinsler cross-ram fuel injection was used. John Greenwood claimed some 680 bhp as 'the norm' for most of his engines. 7800rpm was the rev. limit and the Corvette, with eleven inch wide front and fifteen inch wide rear wheels, weighed in at 2900 pounds.

In 1976, a big block Corvette, built up by the Garcia brothers of Miami, qualified fourth for Daytona, out-qualifying everyone but the Factory BMW team. Amazingly, they finished the twenty-four-hour race just outside the top twenty. Javier Garcia later recalled: "John Greenwood had a problem in qualifying with his engine, so we lined up fourth on the grid. We only went through four rear axles and three gearboxes in that race!"

"That was one fast car. We were timed at over 200mph on the banking at Daytona. At Sebring, we qualified in fourth place again, but mechanical problems dropped us to twenty-ninth at the finish. Later on, we finished in the top ten at the Paul Revere meeting at Daytona in July."

"I built four Corvettes during the seventies. In 1977, we did buy a Greenwood car, but it didn't do so well as the 1976 one!"

Phil Currin, Cliff Gottlob and Peter Knab drove "Fast" Phil's Corvette to 9th place overall at Daytona, but the works-entered BMW 3.0 CSL of Peter Gregg, Brian Redman and John Fitzpatrick was the overall winner. Sebring was worse, the best Corvette placing being eighteenth, twelfth in class.

Phil Currin: "In 1976, at Daytona, we were the first American car home *(in ninth place–Author)*. At Sebring, we had twenty-seven University of Florida students as our pit-crew in three nine-man shifts. It was a disaster! We had a forty-five minute pit-stop as the brake lights failed and no-one knew how to get them working again. In the end, I took a starter button, found a live wire to the brake lights and taped the button onto the transmission tunnel. When I approached turn one, in full view of the timing and scoring, I'd press the button as I hit the brakes. After a while, I found myself pressing the button and forgetting to hit the brakes!"

"Cliff Gottlob was a great co-driver, so easy-going. He came and did one thirty minute practice session on the Thursday and then said: 'Do you mind if I go to Disney World tomorrow? I'll be back on Saturday for the race.'"

"In 1977, I got a call from a sponsor and that started an eight-year relationship before I decided that I was tired of towing all over the country. In 1978, we took pole position at Daytona for the 24-Hour race and came in second in the GTO class. At one time, I had Mark Raffauf, Tom Seibold and George Silbermann on my crew, all ex-University of Florida guys. In 1979, I received two thousand dollars from Arthur Montgomery, the founder of Road Atlanta, for: 'doing the most with the least.' I was very proud of that award."

At Le Mans, Henri Greder's car, the only Corvette to be entered this year, only lasted one hour before engine problems sidelined him.

As Porsche gained a stranglehold on IMSA racing, particularly with the powerful turbocharged Porsche 934s and 935s from 1977 onward, a few stalwarts still came out to do battle with their Corvettes. Phil Currin, Dave Heinz, Rick Thompkins, Ford Smith, Rick Hay and one John Paul (with a Greenwood built GT car), struggled on gamely, having fun but not winning much. At Daytona, John Carusso, Luis Sereix, Emory Donaldson and Lynn St. James did manage an overall sixth place (fourth in the IMSA GT class), but otherwise pickings were slim.

An American built car did win the 1976 and 1977 Championships but this was the tube-framed Dekon Chevrolet Monza of Al Holbert. John Greenwood kept on trying at Le Mans with his wide-bodied "Super-Corvettes" but different problems confounded his ambition to finish year after year.

In 1978, the best Corvette entered in the Daytona 24-Hours was not even classified, so strong was the Porsche domination. To add insult to injury, at Sebring, for once, a Corvette failed to take the GT class, that honor going to the Buick Skylark of Gene Felton and Vince Gimondo. The best Corvette finished two places behind, third in the GTO standings. Dale Kreider and Bruce Davidson finished sixth overall at the Talladega 6-Hours race, whilst Rick Hay and Phil Currin finished eighth overall.

Tony de Lorenzo: "Bill Link Chevrolet sponsored me for the Trans Am series in 1978. We had the pole whenever we ran. The biggest problem we had was with the rules, as our car was built to the very letter of them. I got so fed up being protested for this and that, I went to John Szymanis and pushed, I don't know, some eight hundred bucks at him. (It was a hundred dollars to put in a protest.) 'Here's the deal,' I told him. 'I'm tired of all these protests. There are at least eight cars in this field that I can protest and have them on their trailers and out of here now. Make up your own mind.' That was the end of me being protested!"

At the end of 1978, Corvette fans could at least take pride in the fact that "their" car had won the SCCA Trans Am series in Category 2, the IMSA AAGT class Manufacturers Championship and the SCCA A production and B Stock, plus B prepared and B Stock Ladies Solo 2 National Championships.

Come 1979, no Corvette finished either Daytona or Sebring, but a surprise result was a third place in the El Salvador 6-Hours, a race counting towards the World Challenge for endurance drivers. This result was gained by Javier and Jose Garcia and Luis Sereix in a Greenwood-built car. A Corvette also won the SCCA Trans Am series outright (Category 1), as well as the usual SCCA Championships.

Phil Currin: "In the 1980s, I was driving in IMSA GTO events and winning a few. Then I decided to go Trans Am racing and immediately qualified on the pole for the first race. I retired from that in 1982. Then I came back in 1991 in the Exxon Supreme series with a Camaro and won five out of the ten races. I bought my old '63 split window 'Vette back that I had sold in 1974. I gave it a complete show restoration. In 1994, I took it Vintage racing and did Watkins Glen, Daytona, Road Atlanta, all over again. I was five seconds a lap faster than I'd gone all those years before but of course, the car now had a real race motor and benefited from modern race preparation too."

Always questing for a faster Corvette, Chevrolet produced a mid-engined prototype for the road in 1980. It never made it into production, the management at GM deciding to keep the "standard" front-engined format. Who knows what a race-developed Corvette might have done?

Where the road cars were concerned, 1980 saw the Corvette beginning to claw its way back to being a proper sports car again. In that year, the designers removed over 250 lbs. from the car and improved the aerodynamics. There was also a slightly revised chassis and a new crossmember to support the gearbox. The 4-speed manual gearbox was fitted with higher ratios on first and second gear, to give better fuel consumption. At Chevrolet, all eyes were focussed on the new Corvette being designed with a target date of 1983 set for its introduction.

By 1982, the Corvette had an all-new drive-train, foreshadowing that of the 1984 model but these were truly years of Porsche domination on the track and it would take an all-new model to set Corvette back to winning again.

CHAPTER FOUR

NEW SHAPE, NEW BEGINNING
1984 to 1996

October 23rd, 1988. The "Corvette GTP," with Sarel van der Merwe driving at the race held at the Del Mar Fairgrounds, in San Diego. This was a Lola chassis, number HU-8710/01, and van der Merwe started from third on the grid. The Corvette GTP car was very fast, particularly with the turbocharged V6 engine that Ryan Falconer fitted. Sadly, its reliability and fuel consumption let it down. [Photo: Courtesy of Gordon Barrett.]

Although the 1970s had seen the nadir of the road-going Corvette's fortunes, the 1980s saw a steady climb towards the car's embodiment as "America's sports car." As we have seen, the beginning of the 1980s saw the car shedding weight and becoming more efficient. The new 1984 model year Corvette would take this performance gain to new, higher levels.

We must backtrack a little here, to 1982 in fact. In that year the 350 cubic inch V8 of the Corvette gained a new induction system, called "crossfire injection." This consisted of throttle body injectors, which metered fuel into the airflow through the intake manifold electronically. Together with a redesigned camshaft and stainless steel exhaust headers, this engine produced a net 200 horsepower at just 4,200 rpm and gave the 1982 Corvette better performance than its emissions strangled predecessors.

The new 1984 model was completely redesigned. This was 2" wider, 8.8" shorter and 1.1" lower. The new chassis wheelbase was 2" shorter than the previous model and weight was reduced by another 250lbs. This radical new chassis was composed of a "C" section aluminum backbone, which gave new rigidity to the link between the engine and transmission and the differential. Coupled to this were new aluminum suspension arms, propshaft and cross members, and a new 5-link rear suspension. Top speed was over 140 miles an hour and cornering power with the Z51 package was up to .95G. Despite these reductions in dimensions, this new Corvette was far roomier inside than had been the previous models. This 1984 model Corvette also saw the introduction of Chevrolet's first digital instrumentation, which was only visible to the driver when the ignition was turned on.

The new clean shape of the 1984 Corvette was penned by Jerry Palmer, the Chief Designer for Chevrolet's Studio Three since 1974. Possibly the biggest criticism that could be pointed at the 1984 Corvette was a harsh ride brought on by, perhaps, over-emphasis on good handling. After all, Dave McLelland, the Chief Engineer, was first and foremost a suspension engineer!

The engine was a carry over from the 1982 model with minor improvements to bring the power up to 205 horsepower and torque was quoted at 290lbs/ft. at a mere 2,800rpm. A notable feature of the new car was the fact that aluminum was used for a great many of the suspension and chassis components, enabling a lighter car to be built. That the Corvette was a great sales success was not in doubt: Some 51,547 cars were built and sold.

The 1985 car was virtually identical to the 1984 model and it took until 1986 before the ride deficiency of the 1974 model was addressed and met. The big news for 1986 was the reintroduction of the open top's convertible and the introduction of Bosch ABS II anti-lock braking.

Shown here with its 1953 predecessor, the 1984 Corvette illustrates just how far the car had been developed. [Photo: Courtesy of GM Media Archives.]

Through the 1980s the Corvette substantially took the path of most European designed sports cars, that is it was progressively developed, rather than being dramatically changed in its looks year by year. In fact, it was not until the introduction of the all-new C5 in 1997 that the Corvette's looks changed radically.

IMSA GTP – THE MID-ENGINE CORVETTE RACER

The Corvette GTP car in its final "short tail" version in 1988. Note that now the GTP car has a double element tail in place of the earlier, single-element tail. [Photo: Courtesy of Gordon Barrett.]

The 1984 Chevrolet Corvette GTP (nee Lola) when first introduced. [Photo: Used with permission of GM Media Archives.]

Although it bore almost no relationship to the road-going car, the Corvette GTP of 1984-1988 certainly saw a lot of racing and bore the Corvette name with pride. The GTP Corvette was borne in an effort to raise the Corvette's profile in the public's eye by taking part in the burgeoning IMSA GTP race series, which had begun in 1981 with the Lola T600, driven by Brian Redman, winning the Camel GT Championship. Observing the success of their T600, Lola designed two all-new "customer" GTP cars, known internally as the T710 and T711. The T710 was built to accommodate the Ryan-Falconer Buick-based 3.4 liter V6

The Hendrick Racing Corvette GTP car during a practice session at Mid-Ohio in 1987. [Photo: Courtesy of Gordon Barrett.]

turbocharged engine (originally an Indy car engine from 1980) and the T711 the normally aspirated Chevrolet 350 V8.

Chevrolet initiated the project, specifying that, as far as was possible with a mid-engined GTP car, the bodywork had to resemble their production car.

Road Atlanta, April 1987. Sarel van der Merwe put the Corvette on pole position and set a new lap record but the car lasted just fifty-one laps before it broke. [Photo: Courtesy of Gordon Barrett.]

First of all, Chevrolet gave the only T711 built to Lee Racing of Pennsylvania to test and race. The car was fitted with a 366 cubic inch V8, the largest small-block engine that could be used at the time, and testing at Daytona resulted in the rear wing coming adrift. Although Lew Price brought the car to a halt away from the wall, all the bodywork was torn off. The car was repaired in time for the 1985 Daytona 24-Hours but the car had a dismal showing, retiring after just 160 laps.

At Sebring, the new Corvette GTP car completed just twenty-seven laps before retiring and it was the same story at Charlotte, Mid-Ohio and Watkins Glen. At the second Watkins Glen race, Lew Price and Carson Baird drove the car to eighth place overall. At the Daytona Finale, the car finished in tenth place, although it had taken pole position. (Incidentally, a "production" Corvette had won the SCCA Showroom Stock GT National Championship in 1984.)

The T710 project was put in the hands of Rick Hendrick in 1985, who had previously managed Chevrolet efforts in NASCAR. The V6 engine was now a Chevrolet product, reduced from 229 to 209 cubic inches by shortening the stroke and increasing the bore. Power was quoted at 775bhp with 20psi of boost.

Sarel van der Merwe and David Hobbs were hired as drivers and Ken Howes, previous team chief of the "Kreepy Krauly" March GTP cars that had done well in 1984, took on the same position within the Hendrick team. Goodwrench sponsorship provided the necessary financial backing. In the first race for the team, held at Road America, Hobbs qualified the car eleventh on the grid, but the GTP car retired when the engine failed.

Sarel van der Merwe, in later years, had this to say about driving the Corvette GTP: "In power to weight ratio, the Corvette GTP was as fast as the turbocharged Porsche 917/30. We qualified at over 1,000 horsepower and the chassis was not capable of taking that much power, so qualifying could be pretty scary!"

"Those were the days. The Corvette GTP was one of the most exciting cars I have ever had the privilege to drive, and I wouldn't have missed the experience for the World. I have vivid memories of that Turbocharged V6. I took eight pole positions in 1986. The GTP car was a ball of fire to drive, from the moment you left pit lane until you returned. The V8 version of the Corvette GTP was more manageable but never quite as exciting as the V6 version. Still, the normally aspirated V8 produced almost identical lap times as its lesser power was far more manageable."

"I believe that we still hold the record for the fastest lap at Road America, one of the fastest tracks in the States. Fuel consumption was our problem. Very often, we would beat the Porsches on sheer speed, only to have to make an extra fuel stop, which dropped us down the running."

After the Hendrick Racing Team, the Corvette GTP car was raced a few more times by The Peerless Team. Here is the car at Del Mar, California, in 1988. [Photo: Courtesy of Judy Stropus.]

1985 yielded little as teething troubles saw the Corvette GTPs breaking their engines and gearboxes with distressing frequency. One bright spot was the Daytona Finale, where van der Merwe scored pole position at 1 minute, 38.883 seconds.

1986 was better with two wins plus seven pole positions and three lap records. Although the V6s achieved over 1000 bhp in qualifying trim, the necessary electronic engine management was lacking, resulting in engine destroying detonation. David Hobbs had departed to go to the March/BMW 86G team and his place was taken by Doc Bundy. By season's end, Bundy and van der Merwe were ranked tenth in the IMSA Camel GT Drivers' Championship.

Ken Howes: "The Corvette GTP project was a great opportunity and the engines had enormous power but somehow we suffered reliability problems and, by the time those were cured, the Nissans, amongst others, were even faster. A shame, as it had started out promising so much."

For 1987, the turbocharged engines faced a 3-liter limit and an advanced production based engine management system, made by Chevrolet, was tried. Sadly, it was a failure as the engines proved to be just too thirsty. Even Lotus-developed active ride suspension was tried but, although conferring an advantage, it too failed, needing development.

In 1988, Elliot Forbes-Robinson took Doc Bundy's place besides van der Merwe and the Hendrick team used a T711 chassis, now fitted with a normally aspirated Chevrolet V8 engine, built by Randy Dorton, and using a revised electronic management system. Sadly, other GTP cars such as the Nissan and the TWR Jaguar were superior and Hendrick closed the operation at the end of the year.

Ironically, Lola had supplied the T810, basically a T710 chassis but with the radiator in a different position, to Electramotive for Nissan power and name and this became the dominant GTP car from 1988 to 1991. The Corvette GTP was a brave try but lost its way from 1988 to 1991. Whilst the Nissan V6 engine produced basically as much, if not more, power, the crucial difference between the two Lola chassis was that Electramotive, who managed the Nissan effort of those years, had introduced electronic fuel injection, through the wizardry of Don Devendorf and John Knepp, the proprietors of Electramotive. This not only gave the Nissan GTP ZXT extra fuel mileage, when compared to the Corvette GTP car, it also virtually eliminated engine damage caused by detonation. The Corvette GTP was a brave try but lacked the sort of innovation, which gave Nissan the upper hand in those times.

ZORA RETIRES AND A NEW CHIEF ENGINEER TAKES OVER – 1975 TO 1990

Returning to the production cars, in 1984, the Corvette streetcar changed from an overweight, under-powered, bulbous "Boulevardier," to a new, sleeker, lighter, more powerful Corvette with much improved suspension.

This was Dave McLelland's first Corvette design as Chevrolet's new Chief engineer in charge of the Corvette program. He had taken over from Zora Arkus-Duntov officially on January 1st, 1975, immediately after Arkus-Duntov had retired from the position he had held for nearly twenty years.

David Ramsey McLelland was born in Munising, Michigan and grew up in Detroit. He gained a degree in Mechanical Engineering at Wayne State University in 1959 and then started his first job as a noise and vibration engineer at the Milford Proving Ground. Having gained a Master's Degree in Engineering Mechanics by studying at night, he moved into GM's Vehicle Dynamics Testing in 1968, specifically looking at different suspension and handling set-ups. McLelland joined Chevrolet in 1969 and worked on the 1970 1/2 Camaro and then on John Z. Delorean's Nova/Camaro/Corvette program which, incidentally, Zora Arkus-Duntov had hated. GM later cancelled this.

In 1973, Mclelland spent the year at the Massachusetts Institute of Technology in Boston with forty-nine other mid-career managers. There, at the Sloan School of Management, the fifty students met the industrialists, venture capitalists and other powerful people in Wall Street and Washington, to help prepare them for their next jobs in GM's hierarchy. The result was the new-for-1984 Corvette C4, which, as we have already seen, was a big improvement over the 1968-82 cars. One of its few problem areas was the new four plus three speed gearbox, which appeared to have a mind of its own. The problems were swiftly ironed out by Chevrolet's engineers. The new car also retained the cross-fire twin throttle body injected V8 engine of its predecessor but overall, This new Corvette was a big step forward. In particular, its ride and handling were praised by virtually all the road testers when the new Corvette made its debut.

When McLelland took over from Duntov, he found that, although Duntov had been planning a mid-engined car for the next generation Corvette, customers, when asked, told Chevrolet that they liked the front engined set-up and wanted to stay with it.

The result was the 1984 Corvette, which was a big improvement over the 1968-82 cars. The new four plus three speed gearbox seemed to have a mind of its own, and the car still retained the cross-fire twin throttle body injected V8 engine of its predecessor but Mclelland's new design was seen to be a big improvement, particularly where ride and handling were concerned.

McLelland championed technology and he upgraded his new Corvette over the years, winning the CAFÉ wars and introducing tuned-port fuel injection and Bosch ABS braking long before Chevrolet's rivals did. He re-introduced the roadster, masterminded the ZR-1, improved the Corvette's suspension still further and brought out the six speed gearbox, the LT-1 and traction control.

Dave McLelland was awarded the "Edward N. Cole Award for Engineering Innovation" in 1990 and the Society of American Engineers also cited Mclelland's "successful adaptation of technology to all Corvettes." The new Corvette C4 of the mid 1980s carried on the tradition of the earlier Corvettes in giving the public an attractive, comfortable and fast ride, (but now with much better handling), but at a fraction of the price of the equivalent Ferrari's Porsches, Mercedes et al.

McLelland had to fight hard for some of his Corvette changes. For example, no other Chevrolet car sported the LT-S V8 engine, or Bosch ABS braking. As an engineer, McLelland used engineering science to plan the Corvettes of the future. He designed them with a more upper class customer base in view and made the Corvette equal in engineering to the other supercars of the day such as Ferrari, Porsche, Mercedes etcetera.

From the author's personal point of view, there is no doubt that today's Corvette is every bit as good in performance, ride and handling as any other top marque in the World. The fact that it only costs a fraction of those other marques is a great advantage when choosing just what to buy!

In 1988, Chevrolet took the unprecedented step of producing a series of, ostensibly, stock Corvettes for use in the Corvette Challenge Series, which was put together by John Powell. This series ran through 1988 and 1989 and featured ten races each year, spread across America and Canada. Goodyear and Exxon joined Chevrolet in sponsoring the whole series, which was incidentally shown on ESPN television. The whole thing was a great success, bringing in drivers like Juan Manuel Fangio II, Paul Tracy, Tommy archer, Lou Gillotti and Tommy Kendall, amongst others.

Jim Crist has owned a business selling Corvettes for thirty-five years, in Largo, Florida. Perhaps more than most, he is typical of the amateur race driver who got into Corvette racing in the eighties. He remembered his Corvette racing with great affection.

"In 1954, when I was sixteen and at High School, I bought an old 1954 'Vette, complete with the six cylinder engine. I bought it for a thousand dollars and blew the engine whilst drag racing. I sold the car for five hundred dollars. Guess it's worth a hundred grand now!"

"I've always loved Corvettes and so set up the business, which has always done well. In 1988, I went to the St. Petersburg Grand Prix with a friend. For me, as a beginner to racing, the Trans Am was too fast but it was the first year of the Corvette Challenge. There was Fangio, Lou Gillotti, Tommy Archer, you name it, they were in it. I had my nose pressed to the wire, watching these thundering Corvettes and thought: 'You know, this would be good advertising for my company.'"

"A short time later, the Tampa Bay Car Club put on a show and there was a Corvette Challenge car on display. A dealer owned it and I tried to buy it but the price was too high."

"So I looked in the Corvette magazines and found that Tom Gloy had three Challenge cars for sale. I called him. Two cars had sold and he had just one left. I asked him to hold it

Jim Crist's 1996 Corvette GT1 racer. [Photo: Courtesy of Jim Crist.]

whilst I sent him a cashier's check within 24 hours. He agreed and that's how I got my first Corvette Challenge racecar. When it arrived, I remarked that it had been hit more times than Joe Louis!"

"I went to the Skip Barber School of Racing to get my race license and Terry Earwood, an IMSA driver, was my instructor. I also went to the Akins-White School in Savannah and sent my car to Tommy Morrison to be re-worked and they delivered my Corvette to the track on my last day of instruction."

"At my first race, at Sebring, I placed second and in 1990, I won the SCCA Showroom Stock Pro Championship and remembered my instructor's words: 'All God's male children think that they're born race drivers.' The next year, I won the Central Florida and the Florida Region Championships and won five Championships in all. I did two of the Firehawk races before I moved into racing in an American Sedan."

"I came back to Corvette racing in the GT1 class in 1996 and entered the St. Petersburg Grand Prix. That was the year that Tommy Kendall won everything. It was hard just to get qualified, but we made it. I started twenty-seventh and finished thirteenth. I also won the Florida SCCA GT1 Championship that year."

"For 1997, I bought a Riggins chassis and rebodied it as a C4 Grand Sport and entered the St. Petersburg Grand Prix again. In '98 I went into a sponsorship deal with Ecklers, that took me around a whole host of circuits, including Cleveland, Houston and Miami, with the Trans Am racers."

With the coming of the new Corvette streetcar, Chevrolet engaged Ron Grable to race in the Showroom stock series. "1984 was when we first started doing endurance racing with the showroom stock cars. At least that was what they were supposed to be but they weren't. There was an awful lot of tweaking of the shock absorbers, front to rear brake ratio, swaybars, that sort of stuff."

"We won the Championship for three straight years and so the Corvette was basically legislated out. The cars were still competitive in the top class between Porsche and Chevrolet." In fact, in 1985, Corvettes won all six Showroom Stock endurance races.

In 1987, Tommy Morrison commissioned Protofab to build him a purpose-built race Corvette. A concentrated effort was centered upon this potent new Corvette of the Protofab-Morrison Racing team in the IMSA GTO Championship, introduced at Road Atlanta in the ninth race of the season.

With a sleek body equipped with Chevrolet's new aerodynamic kit for streetcars, and a chassis designed by Bob Riley specifically for Goodyear's new radial tires, the Corvette

Facing Page: Bare bones! The chassis of Jim Crist's GT1 Corvette. [Photos: Courtesy of Jim Crist.]

The First Four Decades of Racing Success

worked well in the hands of Greg Pickett from the outset. He finished second in the rain in the Mobil 1-sponsored car in its second race, and would have won at Sears Point if not for driver heat exhaustion.

One of these Protofab Corvettes raced at Daytona in 1988 but the engine broke, almost within sight of the finish. At Sebring, the car, driven by Wally Dallenbach, Jr. and John Jones came in a superb sixth overall, winning the IMSA GTO class.

In 1989, Wally Dallenbach, Jr. won races at Sebring and Lime Rock in the GTO Championship driving the Protofab Corvette. Dallenbach, Jr. and the Corvette finished up second in the Championship, behind Scott Pruett driving his Lincoln-Mercury XR4Ti. At Sebring, in the Twelve-hour race, Dallenbach and his co-driver, John Jones, finished just twenty laps behind the winning Porsche 962 GTP car driven by Klaus Ludwig and Hans

One of the 1990 World Challenge Corvettes that was entered and raced by The Corvette Center of Connecticut. This photograph was taken at the 1991 St. Petersburg Grand Prix in Florida. Drivers included Shawn Hendricks, Lou Gilotti, Bobby Carradine and others. [Photo: Courtesy of Ray Zitsa.]

Stuck. More impressively, the Corvette beat the winning "Camel Lights" class winner by seven laps.

Reverting to the production Corvettes, in 1989 Chevrolet introduced their most publicized production Corvette ever. This was the LT5/ZR1 and Chevrolet intended this to be a real top of the line, no holds barred, super car. In this they succeeded, having employed Lotus Engineering of Britain to design a 4 camshaft, 32 valve, V8 engine of prodigious power. There was a 6 speed transmission and wheel widths were 9 1/2 inches at the front and 11 inches at the rear, almost the equal of the then current GT racers! Performance was shattering and it was Dave McLelland's crowning achievement before his retirement as Corvette's Chief Engineer in 1990.

Rick Mancuso came back to racing Corvettes in 1989: "I raced a GT1 car in the National Championships. It was a car built to take every advantage the rules could offer. At Road Atlanta, after winning there, we had the car inspected in the tech. bay. The chief tech. looked it over and said: 'Well, the victory stands, but please don't bring it back!'"

In the IMSA GTO Championship, the Corvette slipped back in the standings. New, more powerful Mazda, Nissan and Ford Mustang opposition relegated Andy Pilgrim to an eighth placing in the Exxon Supreme series. At the Corvette's old Sebring stamping ground, Pilgrim's car, co-driven by Bob Smith, could only manage sixteenth overall, sixth in the GTO standings.

Rick Mancuso: "1990, I raced in the Central Division with the GT1 and, in 1999, I entered the Daytona 24-Hours with a basically stock C5 Corvette with the heavy duty springs and shocks package. We were using shaved street tires. We qualified seventy-eighth out of eighty cars. It was an awful experience. We made up over fifty places due to cars in front retiring and, at one point, our crew chief came on the radio to congratulate us. 'You're the first drivers to complete a thousand road racing miles in a modern Corvette.' That was a tough drive."

In 1990, the USAC and FIA sanctioned a series of record attempts at the Firestone test track at Fort Stockton, Texas. There, a Corvette ran for twenty-four hours at an average speed of 175.995mph and the ZR-1 also took six other records from one hundred to five thousand miles and twelve-hour duration.

For 1992, in IMSA competition, life improved for the Corvettes. Shawn Hendricks and Kenny Wallace placed third and fourth respectively, in the Bridgestone Supercar Championship. They were beaten by the Lotus Esprit Turbo of Doc Bundy and the Porsche 930 Turbo of Hurley Haywood. In 1993, the best Corvette in this Championship was that of Sean Roe, who finished sixth. At Sebring that year, the best result was a second in the Invitational GT class for John Heinrici, Stuart Hayner and Andy Pilgrim. At Daytona in 1994, a GTS Nissan 300ZX won outright, covering 707 laps but a Corvette finished in seventh place, albeit 49 laps down.

CHAPTER FIVE

DRAG RACING CORVETTES

Robert "Bones" Balogh bought this old 1958 Corvette in the early 60s and, having fitted a large blower to its small block engine, proceeded to win everything in his class for the next few years. [Photo: Courtesy of Robert Balogh.]

Corvettes have been drag-raced almost since their inception. The idea of fitting a fiberglass body atop a simple ladder frame was made to order, as far as drag racers were concerned.

It would be impossible to attempt to document the amount of "traffic light Grand Prix" that must have taken place around the world by street Corvettes, but in the real world of the quarter-mile strips around the Country, the Corvette has proved a firm favorite, particularly with the "Funnycar" brigade.

Bones Balogh was racing a 1958 Corvette at the dragstrips on the West Coast in the sixties: "I had this early Corvette into which I put a 327 engine. I bolted on a 671 blower and all the guys said: 'That's too big, it'll never work.' But it did. I didn't need so many revs to get the power I needed and we went to Indianapolis and I ran 130 mph at 10.88 to become National Champion."

Above: "Bones" Balogh (left) with his mechanic, Norm Stein, with their impressive bunch of trophies outside the Iskenderian Camshaft factory in 1962. They had just returned from a very successful tour of American drag strips.

Left: "Bones" Balogh standing by his old 1958 drag racing Corvette.
[Photos: Courtesy of Robert Balogh.]

Above: The Corvette had just been unloaded from its open trailer and "Bones" Balogh, crash helmet in hand, awaits his first practice run. [Photo: Courtesy of Robert Balogh.]

Right: Blast off! Ron Nunes gets his Corvette "Funnycar" off the line to take another win [Photo: Courtesy of Cody Coleman.]

"After that, I pretty much ran the 'Vette until there was no-one else to beat, including big John Mazmanian in his '62 'Vette. He was only using a 471 blower and couldn't match me."

"About a year after becoming National Champ, I hurt my engine and was looking at it gloomily at a strip when Mazmanian came over and said: 'Why don't we team up? You've got that old Corvette and I've got a much newer one.' So we did. I sold my Corvette and we put a good motor of mine with the 671 size blower into John's car and beat out all the opposition until we got tired of that and went into a Willy's jeep together, but that's another story…"

Ron Nunes of Danville, California was another drag racer with Corvettes: "I started out in the late fifties with a '32 Ford and raced the guys around here and wound up saying: 'Let's go to a local dragstrip to sort this out.'"

"My first drag racing Corvette was a 1968 car with a Chrysler 454 Hemi in it, supercharged. It would do zero to 168.01 in 8.40 seconds on pump gas. Those Hemis are incredible in the way that they can handle ordinary gas, it's the shape of the combustion chamber that does it. The car had an aftermarket rectangular steel frame with coil over Koni shock absorbers on it and a lighter than standard aftermarket body."

"Just recently, I got into Nostalgia racing with a 1963 split-window Corvette Coupe. It has a 426 Chrysler Hemi that's just magic with a blower fitted. It's a tube-frame car and goes zero to 200 mph in 6.0 seconds. It pulled 3.4 G in low gear and 2.4 G in high."

"When you think about it, it's covering a football field every second at terminal velocity – You couldn't get off your chair and go to close your office door in that six seconds! Sure is a hell of a thrill."

Burn out! Ron Nunes spins the tires in preparation for the next run. [Photo: Courtesy of Cody Coleman.]

Tom McEwen raced a "Corvette" in the seventies and eighties as a "Funnycar," and remembered: "The car wasn't really a Corvette! Oh, sure, it had Corvette-style bodywork but we were using Chrysler Hemi engines. Still, from the outside, it looked like a Corvette and that's what it was entered as."

Perhaps the only places that Corvettes don't seem to have run at are the major ovals (if one discounts Daytona). That's the penalty to be paid when you are, "America's Sportscar," as NASCAR only allows Sedans!

Tuesday, Aug. 28, 1962 — ★ Inglewood Daily News

World's Quickest Corvette Leaves Inglewood to Start National Tour

28 States on Agenda for Racing Team

The recognized world's quickest Corvette, racing out of Inglewood, will leave this week on a coast-to-coast tour covering 28 states and logging over 8,000 miles.

J&J Mufflers and Speed Equipment of Inglewood is sending the racing team of Robert "Bones" Balogh, driver and engine mechanic, and crew chief Norm Stein on the junket to exhibit the fleet 1959 Corvette.

The car has been clocked in the quarter mile from standing start to 129.9 miles per hour in 11.2 seconds.

It has won both the National and American hot rod association titles in the last three months to gain the tag as "world's quickest."

Open Challenge

There is an open challenge of $50 for any Corvette who can better these achievements in a race, according to J&J co-owner Mike Soskin.

The car is equipped with a supercharged Corvette engine featuring an Iskenderian camshaft, aluminum rods and blower drive, a stroked crankshaft, Mickey Thompson forged aluminum pistons, NGK spark plugs and a B&M racing hydramatic transmission. The engine is capable of operating in excess of 9,500 RPM.

Soskin pointed out that the purpose of the tour is for the team to defend its national records and they will be on the road from four to six weeks.

First Stop

First stop will be Indianapolis where the National Hot Rod Association will be conducting its eighth annual championship drags over the Labor Day weekend.

Among the other stops will be Detroit, Minneapolis, West Salem, Ohio, and Washington D.C.

The team of Balogh and Stein have won over 400 races throughout the Western United States and are confident of further success in the east.

OFF ON TOUR — This 1959 Corvette, owned by J&J Muffler and Speed Equipment of Inglewood, leaves this week on a 28-state tour which will cover over 8,000 miles in four to six weeks. The Corvette has been called "world's quickest" by both the National and American hot rod associations.

J & J Muffler and Speed Equipment wish to thank all the manufacturers who contributed their effort and products which enabled us to win the B Modified Sports Car class at the Nationals.

Good luck to Bones-Norm-Bascilk and Wilcox on the remainder of your tour. Watch these winners who are J & J equipt.

World's quickest Corvette T-Shirt & Decal $1.50

Special of the week .. Fiberglass hood scoops from $9.95 painted ....

501 S. LaBrea Ave.   OR 8-0880   Inglewood, Calif.

THE FIRST FOUR DECADES OF RACING SUCCESS

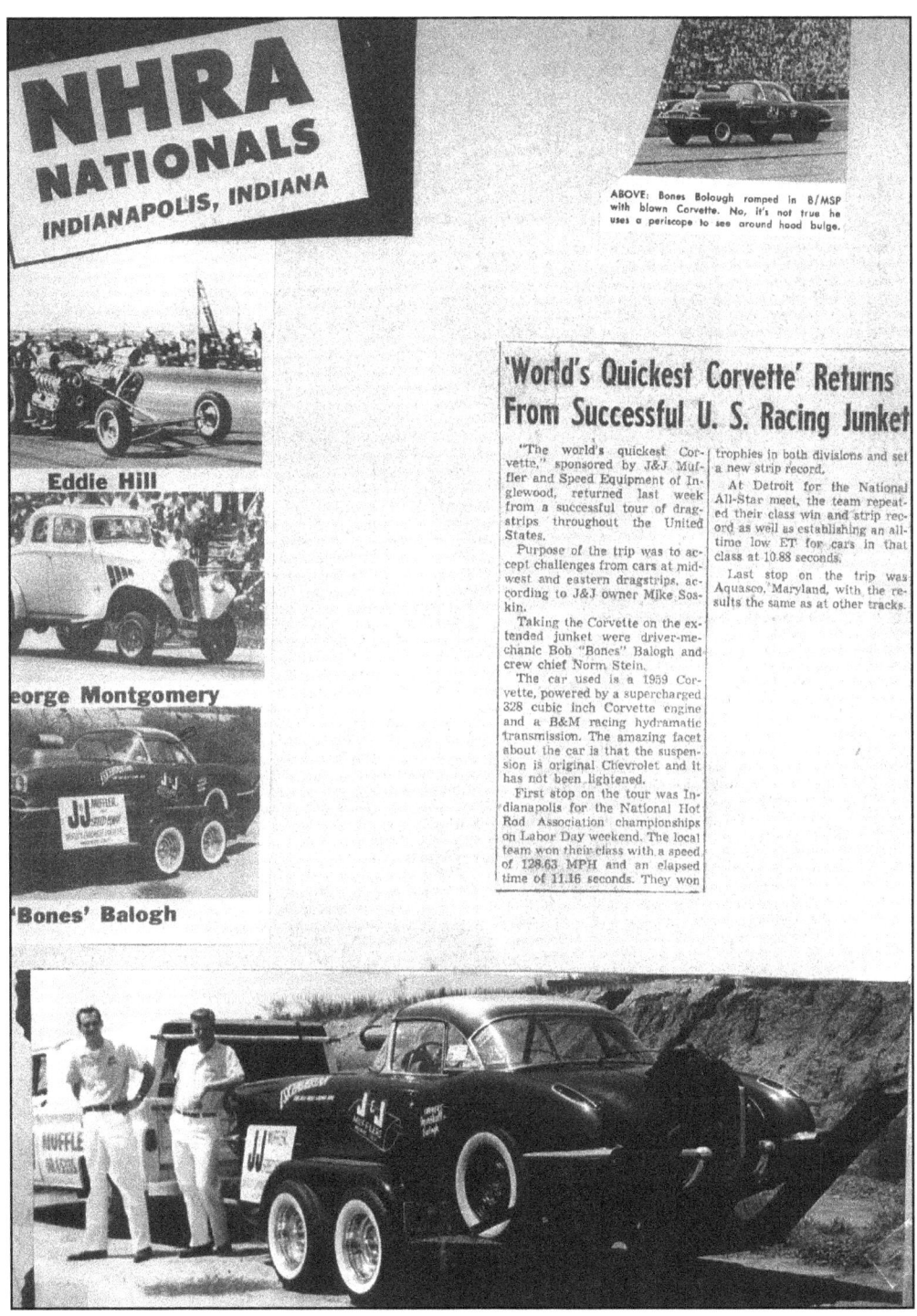

ABOVE: Bones Balough romped in B/MSP with blown Corvette. No, it's not true he uses a periscope to see around hood bulge.

Eddie Hill

George Montgomery

'Bones' Balogh

'World's Quickest Corvette' Returns From Successful U. S. Racing Junket

"The world's quickest Corvette," sponsored by J&J Muffler and Speed Equipment of Inglewood, returned last week from a successful tour of dragstrips throughout the United States.

Purpose of the trip was to accept challenges from cars at midwest and eastern dragstrips, according to J&J owner Mike Soskin.

Taking the Corvette on the extended junket were driver-mechanic Bob "Bones" Balogh and crew chief Norm Stein.

The car used is a 1959 Corvette, powered by a supercharged 328 cubic inch Corvette engine and a B&M racing hydramatic transmission. The amazing facet about the car is that the suspension is original Chevrolet and it has not been lightened.

First stop on the tour was Indianapolis for the National Hot Rod Association championships on Labor Day weekend. The local team won their class with a speed of 128.63 MPH and an elapsed time of 11.16 seconds. They won trophies in both divisions and set a new strip record.

At Detroit for the National All-Star meet, the team repeated their class win and strip record as well as establishing an all-time low ET for cars in that class at 10.88 seconds.

Last stop on the trip was Aquasco, Maryland, with the results the same as at other tracks.

137

Appendix I

THE PRODUCTION CARS

[All photographs in Appendix I – Courtesy of GM Archives.]

1953

Engine:
Overhead-valve cast-iron six, 235.5 cid, bore and stroke 3.56 x 3.93 ins, compression ratio 8:1, 150bhp @4,200rpm.
Chassis:
Box-section ladder-type. IFS via coil springs and wishbones, live rear axle with leaf springs. Wheelbase 102in, overall length 167 ins, track 57/59in front/rear, tires 6.70 x 15in. Chassis numbers: E53F001001 through E53F001300. 300 built.
Transmission:
Standard Powerglide two-speed automatic with floor shift.
Options:
Signal-seeking AM radio $145, heater-demister $91, whitewall tires $25.

1954

Engine:
As per 1953; new camshaft increased power to 155 bhp in mid-model year.
Chassis:
As per 1953. Chassis numbers: E54S001001 through E54S004640. 3,640 built.
Options:
As per 1953, plus windshield washer $12 and parking brake alarm $6.

1955

Engine:
As per 1953, but few six-cylinder engines fitted. Most cars used optional ($134) overhead-valve cast-iron V8, 265cid, bore and stroke 3.75 x 3.00in, CR 8:1, 195bhp @ 5,000rpm.
Chassis:
As per 1953. Chassis numbers: VE55S001001 through VE55S001700. 700 built.
Options:
As per 1954. Electrical system for V8 cars uprated from 6 to 12 volts. 3-speed manual transmission offered for first time. 70-80 cars built with this option.

1956

Engine:
Overhead-valve cast-iron V8, 265cid, bore and stroke 3.75 x 3.00in, CR 9.25:1. 210bhp @ 5,200rpm (225bhp $175, 240bhp $160).
Chassis:
Wheelbase 102in, overall length 168in, track 57/59in front/rear, tires 6.70 x 15in. Chassis numbers: E56S001001 through E56S004467. 3,467 built. Note: Major body redesign.
Transmission:
Three-speed manual gearbox (Powerglide $175).
Options:
Power top $100, power windows $60, windshield washer $11, detachable hardtop $200, signal-seeking AM radio $185, heater-demister $115, whitewall tires $25.

1957

Engine:
Overhead-valve cast-iron V8, 283cid, bore and stroke 3.87 x 3.00in, CR 9.5:1. 220bhp @ 4,800rpm (245bhp $140, 270bhp $170, 250bhp $450, fuel-injection 283bhp $450 or $675 with cold-air induction system).

Chassis:
As per 1956, with optional Positraction $45 and racing suspension $725. Chassis numbers: E57S100001 through E57S106339. 6,339 built.

Transmission:
Three-speed manual gearbox (automatic $175, four-speed gearbox $188).

Options:
Signal-seeking AM radio $185, detachable hardtop $215, power top $130, courtesy light package $8, 15 x 5.5in wheels $14, heater-demister $118, windshield washer $12, parking brake alarm $5, whitewall tires $32, dual carburation $151, two-tone paint $19, Motorola radio $125, electric windows $55.

1958

Engine:
As per 1957 except 230bhp @ 4,800rpm (245bhp $150, f-i 250bhp $484, f-i 290bhp $484).

Chassis:
Wheelbase 102in, overall length 177.2in, track 57/59 ins front/rear, tires 6.70 x 15in. Positraction $48, heavy-duty brakes and suspension $780, available final drive ratios 3.70, 4.11, 4.56:1. Chassis numbers: J58S100001 through J58S109168. 9,168 built.
Note: Body redesigned with dual headlights.

Transmission:
Three-speed manual gearbox (Powerglide $188, four-speed manual $215).

Options:
Power top $140, heater-demister $97, extra cove color $16, detachable hardtop $215, signal-seeking AM radio $144, power windows $59, 15 x 5.5. ins wheels no extra charge, windshield washer $16, whitewall tires $32, courtesy lights $6, parking brake alarm $5.

1959

Engine:
As per 1958 (245bhp $151, 250bhp $484, 270bhp $183, 290bhp $484).

Chassis:
As per 1958 (Positraction $48, HD brakes and suspension $425). Chassis Numbers: J59S100001 through J59S109670. 9,670 built.

Transmission:
As per 1958 plus 4-speed manual (option 685) @ $188.30 extra.

Options:
Power top $140, windscreen washer $16, transistor radio $150, deluxe heater $102, two-tone paint $16, electric windows $59, courtesy lights $6, parking brake alarm $5, sunshades $11, 15 x 15 in. wheels no extra charge, detachable hardtop $237.

1960

Engine:
As per 1958 (230bhp) except CR 9.25:1 (245bhp $151, 270bhp $183, f-i 275/315bhp $484).

Chassis:
As per 1958. Positraction $43, HD brakes and suspension $333. Available final-drive ratios 3.70, 4.11, 4.56:1. Chassis numbers: 00867S100001 through 00867S110261. 10,261 built.

Transmission:
Three-speed manual gearbox (automatic $199, four-speed $188).
Options:
Power top $140, windshield washer $16, signal-seeking transistor radio $138, deluxe heater $102, detachable hardtop $237, two-tone paint $16, electric windows $60, whitewall tires $32, courtesy lights $6, parking brake alarm $5, sunshades $11, special 15 x 5.5 ins wheels no extra charge.

1961

Engine:
As per 1960 except CR 9.5:1 (245bhp $151, 270bhp $183, f-i 275/315bhp $484).
Chassis:
as per 1959 (options as per 1959 plus metallic brakes $38) Chassis Numbers: 10867S100001 through 10867S110939. 10,939 built.
Note: Rear bodywork redesigned with four taillights.
Transmission:
As per 1960.
Options:
Power top $161, windscreen washer $16, signal-seeking transistor radio $138, deluxe heater $102, detachable hardtop $237, two-tone paint $16, electric windows $59, whitewall tires $32, blackwall nylon tires $5, positive crankcase ventilation $5, 24 gallon fuel tank $161, special 15 x 5.5 in. wheels no extra charge.

1962

Engine:
Overhead valve cast iron V8 327cid, bore and stroke 4.00 x 3.25in., CR 10.5:1, 250bhp @ 4,400rpm (300bhp $54, 340bhp $108, f-i 360bhp $484).
Chassis:
As per 1961, direct flow exhaust system no extra charge, metallic brake linings $38, Positraction $43, HD brakes and suspension $333. Chassis Numbers: 20867S100001 through 20867S114531. 14,531 built.
Transmission:
Three speed manual gearbox (automatic $199, four speed $188).

1963

Engine:
Overhead-valve cast-iron V8 327cid, bore and stroke 4.00 x 3.25in, CR 10.5:1, 250bhp @ 4,400rpm (300bhp $54, 340bhp $108, f-i 360bhp $430).
Chassis:
Steel perimeter frame with independent suspension front and rear, the latter via three-link with double-jointed open drive-shafts at either side, control arms and trailing radius rods with single transverse leaf spring. Wheelbase 98in, overall length 175.2in, track 56.8/57.6in front/rear, tires 6.70 x 15in. Sintered metallic brake linings $38, off-road exhaust system $38, RPO Z06 performance package for coupe (including metallic power brakes, HD shock absorbers, stabilizer bars, knock-off aluminum wheels, Positraction, four-speed, 260bhp engine

$1,818, Positraction $43. Available final-drive ratios 3.08, 3.36, 3.55, 3.70, 4.11, 4.56:1. Chassis numbers: 30867S100001 through 30867S121513. 21,513 built. Note: "Sting Ray" introduced. Body and chassis completely redesigned.
Transmission:
Three-speed manual gearbox (automatic $199, four-speed $188).
Options:
Power brakes $43, power steering $73, air conditioning $422, hardtop $237, signal-seeking transistor radio $138, electric windows $60, whitewall tires $32, blackwall Nylon tires $16, HD brakes with metallic linings $38, Sebring Silver paint $81, woodgrain steering wheel $15, aluminum knock-off wheels $323, AM-FM radio $174, tinted windshield $11, tinted glass $16, leather seat trim $81.

1964

Engine:
As per 1963 (300bhp $54, 364bhp $108, f-i 365bhp, $538).
Chassis:
As per 1963. Chassis Numbers: 40867S100001 through 40867S12222. 22,229 built.
Transmission:
As per 1963.
Options:
As per 1963 plus 36 gallon fuel tank for coupe $202, reversing lamps $11.

1965

Engine:
As per 1963 (other 327 engines: 300bhp $54, 365bhp $129, f-i 375bhp $538; L78 396cid 425bhp $292).
Chassis:
As per 1963 except standard tires now 7.75 x 15in., four wheel disc brakes standard, special front and rear suspension $38, Positraction $43, side-mounted exhaust system $135. Chassis Numbers: 194675S100001 through 194675S123562. 23,562 built.

Transmission:
as per 1963 (special HD close-ratio four speed manual gearbox $237).
Options:
As per 1963 plus teak wood steering wheel $48, AM-FM radio with power antenna $237, 'goldwall' tires $51, telescopic steering column $43. Knock-off wheels $333.

1966

Engine:
As per 1963 except 300bhp @ 5,000rpm (350bhp $105, L39 427 cid, 390bhp $181, L72 427cid, 425bhp $312, transistor ignition system $73). Fuel-injected engines dropped.
Chassis:
As per 1965. Chassis Numbers: 194676S100001 through 19467S127720. 27,720 built.

1967

Engine:
As per 1963 (350bhp $105, L36 427cid 390bhp $200, L68 427cid 400bhp $306, L71 427cid 435bhp $437, aluminum cylinder heads for L71 $368).
Chassis:
As per 1963 except standard tires now 7.75 x 15in, four-wheel disc brakes standard, special front and rear suspension $38, Positraction $43, side-mounted exhaust system $135. Available final-drive ratios 3.08, 3.36, 3.55, 3.70, 4.11:1. Chassis numbers: 194677S100001 through 194677S122940. 22,940 built.
Transmission:
As per 1963 (special HD close-ratio four-speed gearbox $237).
Options:
Power brakes $42, power steering $95, air conditioning $413, front shoulder belts $26, 36-gallon fuel tank for coupe $198, tinted windows $16, tinted windshield $11, headrests $42, heater-demister $98, power windows $58, AM-FM radio $173, black vinyl roof cover $53, leather upholstery $79, speed warning indicator $11, telescopic steering

wheel $42, four-ply whitewall tires $31, red stripe Nylon tires $47, hardtop $231.

1968

Engine:
As per 1967.
Chassis:
As per 1967, wheelbase 98in, overall length 182.5in, track 58.7/59.4in front/rear, tire size F70–15. Available rear axle ratios 2.73, 3.08, 3.36, 3.55, 4.11:1. Chassis numbers: 194678S411010 through 194678S428566. 28,566 built.
Note: "Sting Ray" body extensively redesigned.
Transmission:
As per 1967 (HD gearbox $263, Turbo-Hydramatic $226. Automatic transmission changed from 2-3-speeds.
Options:
Power brakes $42, power steering $95, air conditioning $413, deluxe shoulder belts $25, rear window demister $32, tinted windows $16, tinted windshield $11, head restraints $42, HD power brakes $384, power windows $58, AM-FM radio $173, with stereo $278, black vinyl roof $53, leather seats $79, speed warning indicator $11, adjustable steering wheel $42, detachable hardtop $232, wheel covers $58, red stripe F70–15 tires $31, white stripe tires $32, alarm system $26.

1969

Engine:
Overhead valve V8, 350cid, bore and stroke 4.00 x 3.48in, CR 10.25:1, 300bhp @ 4,800rpm (L36 427 cid 400bhp $326, L71 427cid 435bhp $437, L89 427cid, 435bhp with aluminum heads $832).
Chassis:
As per 1968, steering column lock standard. Chassis Numbers: 19469S700001 through 194679S738762. 38,762 built.
Transmission:
As per 1968 (HD gearbox $290).
Options:
As per 1968.

1970

Engine:
As per 1969 (350bhp $158, LT1 350cid 370bhp $448, LS5 454cid 390bhp $290, LS7 454cid 460bhp $3,000).
Chassis:
As per 1969. Transistor ignition $64, special suspension $29, Positraction $12, HD clutch $63. Available final drive ratios 2.73, 3.08, 3.36, 3.55, 4.11, 4.56:1. Chassis Numbers: 194670S400001 through 194670S417316. 17,316 built.
Note: Body equipped with fender flares.
Transmission:
Four speed manual gearbox (automatic no extra charge, close ratio four speed no extra charge, HD four speed $95).
Options:
As per 1969.

1971

Engine:
Overhead valve cast iron V8, 350cid, bore and stroke 4.00 x 3.48in, CR 8.5:1, 270bhp @ 4,800rpm (350bhp $483, LS5 454cid 365bhp $295, LS6 454cid 425bhp $1,221).
Chassis:
As per 1969 (ZR1 package: HD brakes, close ratio four speed, special front stabilizer bar, special springs and shock absorbers, transistorized ignition

and LT1 engine $1,010; ZR2: all ZR1 except LS6 engine $1,747), side-mounted exhaust system $117. Chassis Numbers: 194671S100001 through 194671S121801. 21,801 built.
Transmission:
As per 1970 (HD gearbox $100).
Options:
Power brakes $48, power steering $116, air conditioning $465, alarm system $32, HD battery $16, deluxe shoulder belts $42, rear window demister $42, AM-FM radio $178, with stereo $283, black vinyl roof cover $63, tilt steering wheel $84, white stripe tires $30, white letter tires $44, custom trim $158, custom wheel cover $63, power windows $85.

1972

Engine:
As per 1971 except 200bhp @ 5,500rpm (255bhp $483, LS5 454cid 270bhp $295).
Chassis:
As per 1969. ZR1 package with 255 bhp $1,010. Chassis Numbers: 1Z67K2S500001 through 1Z67K2S527004. 27,004 built.
Note: Last to feature chrome bumpers.
Transmission:
As per 1971. Automatic no extra charge with standard engine, $97 extra with others, not available with 454; close ratio four speed no extra charge.
Options:
As per 1971 except alarm system standard.

1973

Engine:
Overhead-valve cast-iron V8, 350cid, bore and stroke 4.00 x 3.48in, CR 8.5:1, 190bhp (net) @ 4,400rpm (250bhp $299, LS4 454cid 275bhp $250).
Chassis:
As per 1968, steering column lock standard. ZR1 package with 255bhp $1,010. Plus energy-absorbing front bumper. Off-road suspension and brake package $369. Chassis numbers: 1Z67J3S400001 through 1Z67J3S434464. 34,464 built.

Transmission:
Four-speed manual gearbox (automatic no extra charge with standard engine, $97 extra with others, not available with 454, close-ratio four-speed no extra charge, HD gearbox $100.
Options:
Power brakes $48, power steering $116, air conditioning $465, HD battery $16, deluxe shoulder belts $42, rear window demister $42, AM-FM radio $178, with stereo $283, black vinyl roof cover $63, tilt steering wheel $84, white strip tires $30, white letter tires $44, custom trim $158, custom wheel cover $63, power windows $85, plus cast-aluminum bolt-on wheels $175.

1974

Engine:
Overhead-valve cast-iron V8 350cid, bore and stroke 4.00 x 3.48in, CR 9:1, 250bhp @ 5,200rpm (250bhp $299, LS4 454cid 270bhp $250).
Chassis:
Wheelbase 98in, overall length 185.5in, tires GR70–15 (off-road suspension and brake package $400, Gymkhana suspension $7). Chassis numbers: 1Z67J4S400001 through 1Z67J4S437502. 37,502 built.
Transmission:
Four-speed manual gearbox (automatic no extra

charge with standard engine, $97 extra with others, not available with 454, close-ratio four-speed no extra charge, HD gearbox $100.
Options:
Power brakes $49, power steering $117, air conditioning $467, custom interior $154, power windows $83, custom shoulder belts $41, detachable hardtop $267, vinyl-covered hardtop $329, rear window demister $41, tilt steering column $82, white stripe radial tires $32, white letter radial tires $45, dual horns $4, AM-FM stereo radio $276, AM-FM radio $173, HD battery $15, map light $5, cast-aluminum wheel trim $175.

1975

Engine:
As per 1974 except CR 8.5:1, 165bhp @ 3,800rpm, catalytic convertor, High Energy ignition system (205bhp $335).
Chassis:
As per 1974; suspension options deleted. Chassis Numbers: 1Z67J5S400001 through 1Z67J5S438465. 38,465 built.
Transmission:
as per 1974.
Options:
As per 1974; cast aluminum wheel trim deleted.

1976

Engine:
As per 1975 except 185bhp (220bhp $335). Z07 option with L82 engine: 205bhp.
Chassis:
As per 1975. Chassis Numbers: 1Z37L6S400001 through 1Z37L6S446558. 46,558 built.
Note: Coupes only until 1986.
Transmission:
As per 1975.
Options:
As per 1975 except aluminum wheels now offered @ $321.

1977

Engine:
As per 1974 except CR 8.5:1, 185bhp catalytic convertor, High Energy ignition system (210bhp $495).
Chassis:
Wheelbase 98in, overall length 185.5in, tires GR70–15B. Chassis numbers: 1Z37L7S400001 through 1Z37L7S449213. 49,213 built.
Transmission:
Four-speed manual gearbox (automatic no extra charge with standard engine, $97 extra with others, not available with 454, close-ratio four-speed no extra charge, HD gearbox $100.
Options:
AM-FM stereo radio $281, with tape deck $414, aluminum road wheels $321, power windows $100, glass canopy roof $200, speed control, tilt steering wheel $165, air conditioning $450. (Leather seats, power steering and power brakes now standard.)

1978

Engine:
As per 1977 (220bhp $525).
Chassis:
As per 1977. Chassis numbers: 1Z87L8S400001 through 1Z87L8S440274. 1Z87L8S900001 through

1Z87L8S906502 (pace car). 40,274 standard and 6,502 pace car replicas built.
Note: Body redesigned with "fastback" rear end.
Transmission:
As per 1977.
Options:
AM-FM stereo radio $220, with tape deck $439, with CB $525, aluminum road wheels $345, tilt steering wheel $178, removable glass roof panels $349, air conditioning $450; also power windows, rear window demister, speed control, power door locks.

1979

Engine:
As per 1978 except 195bhp (225bhp $595).
Chassis:
As per 1978. Chassis numbers: 1Z8789S400001 through 1Z8789S453807. 53,807 built.
Transmission:
As per 1978.
Options:
As per 1978.

1980

Engine:
As per 1979 (230bhp $595), also overhead valve cast iron V8, 305cid, bore and stroke 3.73 x 3.48in, 180bhp for California.
Chassis:
As per 1979. Chassis numbers: 1Z878AS400001 through 1Z878AS440614. 40,614 built.

Transmission:
As per 1979.
Options:
As per 1979.

1981

Engine:
As per 1980 but 305 cubic inch engine dropped.
Chassis:
As per 1980, transverse fiberglass monoleaf rear spring on models with automatic. Chassis numbers: 1G1AY8764BS400001 through 1G1AY8764BS431611 (St. Louis). 1G1AY8764B5100001 through 1G1AY8764B5108995 (Bowling Green). 40,606 built.
Transmission:
As per 1980.
Options:
As per 1978 plus roof-mounted luggage carrier $144.

1982

Engine:
Overhead-valve cast-iron V8 with Throttle-Body ('Cross-fire') fuel injection, 350cid, bore and stroke 4.00 x 3.48in, 200bhp @ 4,300rpm.
Chassis:
As per 1978, transverse fiberglass monoleaf rear spring on models with automatic. Chassis numbers: 1G1AY8786C5100001 through 1G1AY8786C5125407. 25,407 built.
Transmission:
Three-speed automatic only.
Options:
Aluminum road wheels $458, power seats $197, power door locks $155, luggage rack $144, cruise control $165, removable roof panels $443, custom paint $438; also rear window demister, AM-FM stereo with tape and/or CB.

1983

1983 Corvettes were built and chassis numbered. They were driven by the motoring press at the "long lead" Corvette press preview at Riverside Raceway in December 1982. However, because of its late introduction in March 1983 and because the new Corvette met all 1984 Government requirements, Chevrolet took the decision not to include the 1983 model designation. The 1983 Corvettes were not released for sale to the public and, officially, 1983 Corvettes do not exist.

1984

Engine:
Overhead-valve cast-iron V8, 350cid, bore and stroke 4.00 x 3.48in, 205bhp @ 4,300rpm.
Chassis:
Unequal length A-arms, transverse fiberglass leaf spring, tubular shock absorbers and anti-sway bar front; upper and lower trailing arms, lateral arms, tie rods, half-shafts, transverse fiberglass leaf spring, tubular shock absorbers and anti-sway bar rear; 11.5in vented disc brakes front and rear, vacuum-assisted; cast-alloy road wheels, 15in standard, 16in optional; rack-and-pinion power-assisted steering, overall ratio 13:1, two turns lock-to-lock. Wheelbase 96in, overall length 176.5in, overall width 71in, height 46.9in. Chassis numbers: 1G1AY0781E5100001 through 1G1AY0781E5151547. 51,547 built.
Note: car completely redesigned.
Transmission:
Four-speed manual gearbox with computer-controlled overdrive standard.
Options:
To include all usual Corvette equipment plus electrically adjustable rear view mirrors, Z51 handling package (HD suspension, aluminum prop-shaft and half-shafts, 16 ins wheels and tires. Estimated base price FOB Detroit $24,000.

1985

Engine:
230bhp @ 4,000rpm; new heavy-duty cooling system. GM multi-port fuel injection.
Chassis:
Cast-alloy road wheels, 9.5in. front and rear; gas pressurized Delco-Bilstein shock absorbers. Spring rates lowered by 26/25% front rear. Heavy-duty 8.5in ring gear differential in manual shift models. Chassis Numbers: 1G1YY0787F5100001 through 1G1YY0787F5139729. 39,729 built.
Transmission:
As for 1984.
Options:
As for 1984 plus RPO Z51.

1986

Engine:
Overhead-valve cast-iron V8, 350cid, bore and stroke 4.00 x 3.48in, 230-235bhp.
Chassis:
Unequal length A-arms, transverse fiberglass leaf spring, tubular shock absorbers and anti-sway bar front; upper and lower trailing arms, lateral arms, tie rods, half-shafts, transverse fiberglass leaf spring, tubular shock absorbers and anti-sway bar rear; 11.5in vented disc brakes front and rear, vacuum-assisted; cast-alloy road wheels, 15in standard, 16in optional; rack-and-pinion power-assisted steering, overall ratio 13:1, two turns lock-to-lock. Wheelbase 96.2in, overall length 176.5in, overall width 71in, height 46.7in. ABS braking introduced. Chassis numbers: 1G1YY0789G5100001 through 1G1YY0789G5127794 (coupes). 1G1YY6789G5900001 through 1G1YY6789G5907315 (convertibles). 27,794 coupes and 7,315 convertibles built.
Note: Convertible re-introduced.
Transmission:
Four-speed manual gearbox with computer-controlled overdrive standard. Automatic available.
Options:
To include all usual Corvette equipment plus electrically adjustable rear view mirrors, Z51 handling package (HD suspension, aluminum prop-shaft and half-shafts, 16in wheels, tires.

1987

Engine:
240bhp @ 4,000rpm, compression ratio 9.5:1, torque 345lb./ft. @ 3,200rpm, roller-type lifters, raised rail rocker arm covers, relocated spark plugs.

Chassis:
As per 1986. Calloway twin turbo engine package could be ordered through dealers as RPO B2K. Handling package RPO Z52 combined elements of RPO Z51 with softer suspension of base model. Chassis Numbers: 1G1YY2182H5100001 through 1G1YY2182H5130632. 30,632 built.

Transmission:
As per 1986.

Options:
As per 1986.

1988

Engine:
As per 1987. Calloway twin-turbo: 382bhp, 562lb/ft. torque.

Chassis:
As per 1987 with new 6 slot wheels. New dual piston front brakes. Chassis Numbers: 1G1YY2182J5100001 through 1G1YY2182J5122789. 22,789 built.

Transmission:
As per 1986.

Options:
As per 1986.

1989

Engine:
Overhead-valve cast-iron V8, 350cid, bore and stroke 4.00 x 3.48in, 245bhp.

Chassis:
Unequal length A-arms, transverse fiberglass leaf spring, tubular shock absorbers and anti-sway bar front; upper and lower trailing arms, lateral arms, tie rods, half-shafts, transverse fiberglass leaf spring, tubular shock absorbers and anti-sway bar rear; 11.5in vented disc brakes front and rear, vacuum-assisted; cast-alloy road wheels, 15in standard, 16in optional; rack-and-pinion power-assisted steering, overall ratio 13:1, two turns lock-to-lock. Wheelbase 96.2in, overall length 176.5in, overall width 71in, height 46.7in. Chassis numbers: 1G1YY2186K500001 through 1G1YY2186K526328. 26,328 built.

Transmission:
Four-speed manual gearbox with computer-controlled overdrive standard. Automatic available. 6-speed gearbox available @ no extra cost.

Options:
To include all usual Corvette equipment plus six-speed manual gearbox (MN6), Z51 handling package (HD suspension, aluminum prop-shaft and half-shafts, 16in wheels and tires.

1990

Engine:
As 1989, except new Lotus 4-camshaft L89 375bhp available with ZR-1 Corvette (special performance package) coupe only.

Chassis Numbers:
1G1YY2380L5100001 through 1G1YY2380L5120597. 20,597 built.
ZR-1: 1G1YZZ23J6L5800001 through 1G1YZZ23J6L5803049. 3,049 built.

1991

Chassis Numbers:
1G1YY2386M5100001 through 1G1YY2386M5118595. 18,595 built.
ZR-1: 1G1YZ23J6M5800001 through 1G1YZ23J6M5802044. 2,044 built.
Note: Restyled rear bodywork similar to 1990 ZR-1.

1992

Engine:
New LT-1. 300bhp @ 5,000rpm. 330lb./ft. torque @ 4,000rpm.
Chassis Numbers:
1G1YY23P6N5100001 through 1G1YY23P6N5119977. 19,977 built.
ZR-1: 1G1YZ23J6N5800001 through 1G1YZ23J6N58 00502. 502 built.

1993

Engine:
As per 1992, except ZR-1 up to 405bhp.
Chassis Numbers:
1G1YY23PXP5100001 through 1G1YY23PXP5121142. 21,142 built.
ZR-1: 1G1YZ23J3P5800001 to 1G1YZ23J3P58 00488. 488 built.

1994

Engine:
As per 1993.
Chassis Numbers:
1G1YY22P9R5100001 through 1G1YY22P9R5122882. 22,882 built.
ZR-1: 1G1YZ22J9R5800001 to 1G1YZ22J9R58 00448. 448 built.

1995

Engine:
Overhead-valve cast-iron V8, 350cid, bore and stroke 4.00 x 3.48in, 300bhp/ZUD 405bhp.
Chassis:
As for 1989. Chassis numbers:
1G1YY22P7S5100001 through 1G1YY22P7S5120294. 20,294 built.
ZR-1: 1G1YZ22J0S5800001 through 1G1YZ22JOS5800448. 448 built.
Transmission:
As for 1989. 4-speed automatic transmission redesigned with electronic controls.
Options:
To include all usual Corvette equipment plus six-speed manual gearbox (MN6), Z51 handling package (HD suspension, aluminum prop-shaft and half-shafts, 16in wheels and tires. Z07/ZR-1: Larger brakes fitted to all models.

1996

Engine:
Overhead-valve cast-iron V8, 350cid, bore and stroke 4.00 x 3.48in, 300bhp/ZXD 330bhp. (RPO LT4.)

Chassis:
As for 1995. Chassis numbers:
1G1YY22PST5100001 through 1G1YY22PST5120536. 20,536 built. Grand Sport: 1G1YY225ST5600001 through 1G1YY225ST5601000. 1,000 built.
Transmission:
As for 1995.
Options:
To include all usual Corvette equipment plus six-speed manual gearbox (MN6), Z51 handling package (HD suspension, aluminum prop-shaft and half-shafts, 16in wheels and tires. Price $37,225 for coupe, $45,060 for convertible.

For a car to be able to run in International World Championship races, it has to have what are known as Homologation Papers. These papers specify how many cars must be built to the same specification, and exactly what is and what is not allowed in terms of tuning the basic car.

Overleaf are some extracts from the 1965 "big block" Chevrolet 427 Corvette Homologation Papers.

Appendix II

HOMOLOGATION PAPERS

0 OCT. 1965

AUTOMOBILE COMPETITION COMMIT. **F.I.A.** Recognition N° **523**
FOR THE UNITED STATES, FIA, INC. Group ... **III**
NEW YORK 16, N.Y.

FEDERATION INTERNATIONALE DE L'AUTOMOBILE

Form of recognition in accordance with
Appendix J to the International Sporting Code

Manufacturer .. CHEVROLET.   Cylinder-capacity ..6997....cm3 ...427...in3
Serial N° of chassis 194376S100001   Model Corvette 19437 Coupe
           engine F------IP   Manufacturer ....Chevrolet
Recognition is valid from ....   Manufacturer ....Chevrolet
                                     .... List ...

The manufacturing of the model described in this recognition form was started
on ..Sept. 7..19 65 and the minimum production of ..500... identical cars, in
accordance with the specifications of this form was reached on Sept.28.. 19 65

Photograph A , 3/4 view of car from front

The vehicle described in this form has been subject to the following amendments :

Variants   Normal evolution of the type
on ....19 .. rec.N°...... List ..... on ....19 .. rec.N° ....List.....
on .... 19 .. rec.N° ..... List ..   on ....   19 .. rec.N° ....List ....
on ....19 .. rec.N° ..... List ......on ...... 19 .. rec.N° ....List ..
on ....19 .. rec.N° ..... List....... on ....19 .. rec.N° ....List .
on ....19 .. rec.N° ..... List ..   on ....19 .. rec.N° .. .. List .....

Stamp and signature of the WM. FLEMING   Stamp and signature of the F.I.A.
National Sporting Authority EXECUTIVE DIRECTOR
                            ACCUS, FIA, INC.
                            433 MAIN STREET
                            STAM...

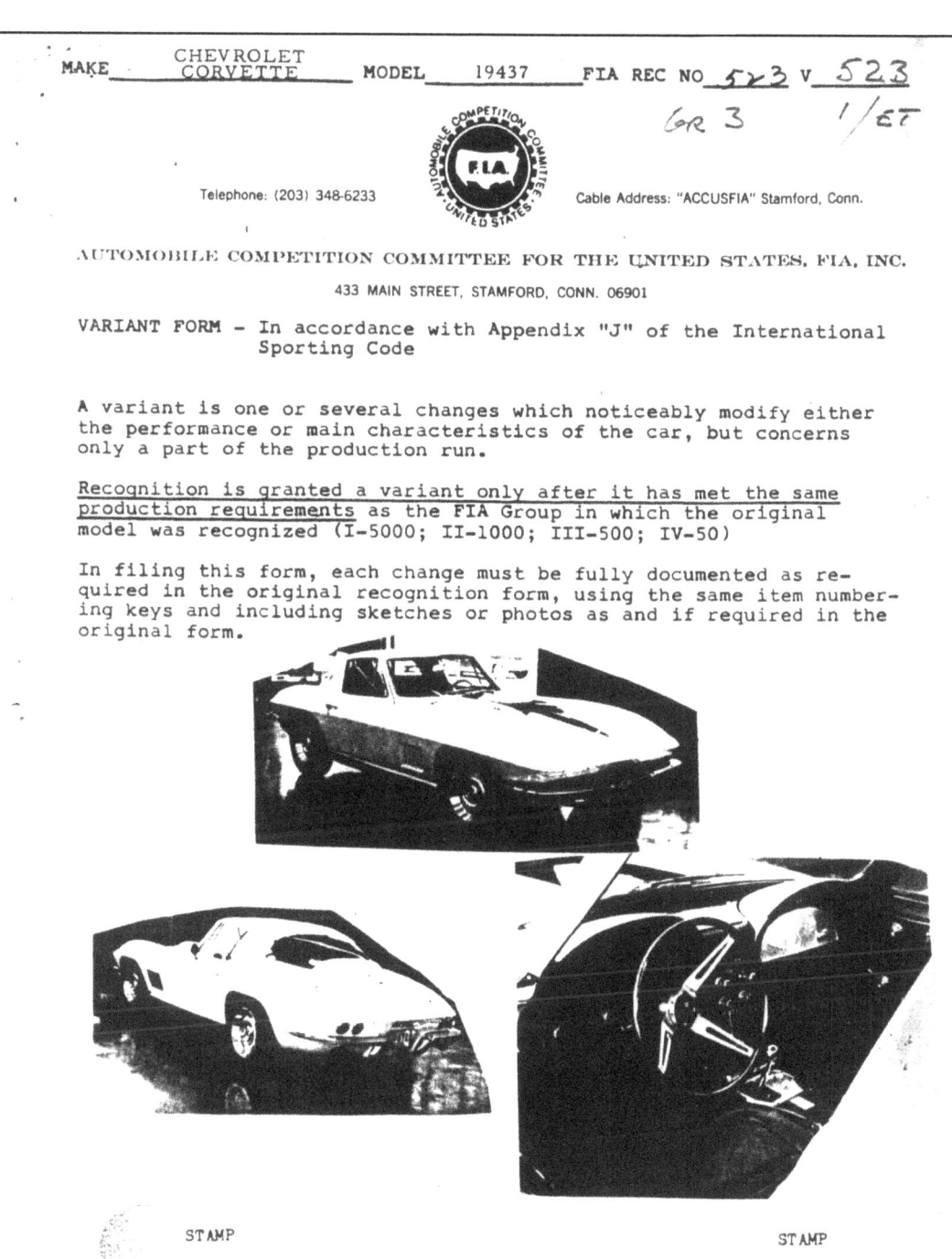

MAKE __CHEVROLET CORVETTE__ MODEL __19437__ REC. NO. __523__ V

The following items are affected - otherwise same as original:

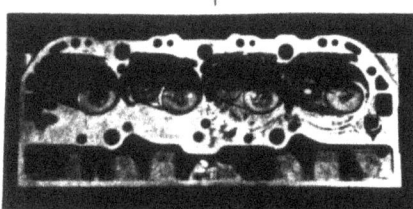
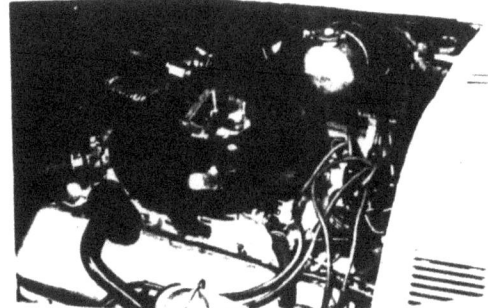

NEW CAM DATA FOR CAM 3879605

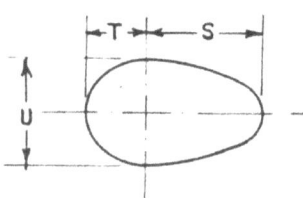

Inlet Cam
S - .94429/.94629 in.   23.985/24.036 mm.
T - .61572/.61772 in.   15.639/15.690 mm.
U - 1.23144/1.23544 in. 31.279/31.380 mm.

Exhaust Cam
S - .94429/.94629 in.   23.985/24.036 mm.
T - .60311/.60511 in.   15.319/15.370 mm.
U - 1.20622/1.21022 in. 30.638/30.740 mm.

9. <u>Weight</u> Total weight of the car with water, oil but without fuel
    1259 Kg.   2778 lbs.

139. Cylinder head material — Aluminum.

195. Material of exhaust manifold — Steel tubing.

196. Diameter of exhaust valves. 46.76 mm. 1.840 inches.
     Battery — Trunk mounted.
     STAMP   **STAMP**

(2)

```
Make Chevrolet Corvette        Model 1943⁷           F.I.A. Rec. N° 323
```

IMPORTANT - the underlined items must be stated in two measuring systems, one of which must be the metric system. See conversion table hereafter.

CAPACITIES AND DIMENSIONS

1. Wheelbase   2489.2   mm   98.0   inches
2. Front track   1480.8   mm   58.3   inches *
3. Rear track   1498.6   mm   59.0   inches *
4. Overall length of the car   cm   175.1   inches
5. Overall width of the car   cm   67.3   inches
6. Overall height of the car   cm   49.7   inches
7. Capacity of fuel tank (reserve included)   75.7   ltrs
            20 Gallon US   Gallon Imp.
8. Seating capacityy 2

@ 9. Weight, total weight of the car with normal equipment, water, oil and spare wheel but without fuel nor repair tools :

~~1409~~   kg   ~~3106~~   lbs   cwt
 1370   3020   FEB 1 1961

*) Differences in track caused by the use of other wheels with different rim widths must be stated when recognition is requested for the wheels concerned. Specify ground clearance in relation to the track and give drawing of two easily recognizable points at front and rear at which measurements are taken. These ground clearance dimensions are only for information when checking the track and can in no way affect the eligibility of the car.

With optional 15X7 wheels, front tread 58.9 inches; rear tread 59.7 inches. Measurement taken between centerlines of tires.

CONVERSION TABLE

1 inch/pouce   - 2.54 cm   1 quart US   - 0.9464 ltrs
1 foot/pied   - 30.4794 cm   1 pint (pt)   - 0.568 ltrs
1 square inch/pouce carré   - 6.452 cm2   1 gallon Imp.   - 4.546 ltrs
1 cubic inch/pouce cube   - 16.387 cm3   1 gallon US   - 3.785 ltrs
1 pound/livre (lb)   - 453.593 gr.   1 hundred weight (cwt) - 50.802 kg

@ Official weight when including RPO and delete   Page 5
  optional equipment - 2851 lb, 1293 kg.

Name of Manufacturer _____Chevrolet Motor Division_____

Name of Model _____Corvette (19437)_____

Manufacturer's Reference No. of Application ___19437-66___

We certify that in excess of __500__ cars identical with the basic specifications as well as in excess of __500__ cars as modified by listed optional equipment stated in this application were completed on __September 28, 1965__. Production commenced on __September 7, 1965__. Cars conforming to these specifications may be identified by Chassis Nos. beginning with __194376S100001__ and Engine Nos. __F--IP__.

Name of Company or Division ___Chevrolet Motor Division___

By _____
Title Staff Engineer, Corvette Engine and Chassis

By _____
Title Chief Special Products Engineer

G. WM. FLEMING
EXECUTIVE DIRECTOR
ACCUS, FIA, INC.
433 MAIN STREET
STAMFORD, CONN. 06901

APPENDIX III

GREENWOOD CORVETTES

Two of the most famous of John Greenwood's wide bodied Corvettes, the "Spirit of Le Mans 76" and the "Spirit of Sebring 76", at the start/finish line at Sebring Raceway. [Photo: Courtesy of Steve Golden.]

Due to John Greenwood's success with his wide-bodied big block Corvettes, John set up a Company called "Greenwood Racing" and fabricated parts that were sold to anybody who wished to modify their Corvette, either for the road or for full competition.

In the next few pages can be found a road test carried out by *Road & Track* magazine of Greenwood's spectacular "Spirit of Sebring '76" car, owned today by Steve Golden. [Reproduced with the kind permission of *Road & Track*.]

Following this are a few pages from Greenwood Racing's 1976 catalog to show the range of parts that could be supplied.

Photographs of Greenwood's shop, during the 1970s, can also been seen.

PHOTOS BY BILL WARNER

CORVETTE & SUPER CORVETTE

John Greenwood helps us test a stock Corvette and his 221-mph race car

FEW CARS IN the history of American sports-car racing have won more victories than the Chevrolet Corvette. And in the past six years no person has done more to earn the title of Mr Corvette than John Greenwood. Greenwood started building and running his own Corvettes in 1969, winning the SCCA A Production championship in 1970 and 1971. During 1972 and 1973, while running under B.F. Goodrich sponsorship, Greenwood's T/A radial-equipped Vette scored some impressive victories against competitors who had the advantage of running on stickier racing tires. Engine problems dashed Greenwood's hopes for a 1972 Le Mans class win, but the car's potential was clearly evident as it qualified fastest for the GT class—on T/A street tires no less!

With a new car again on racing rubber for 1974, Greenwood's Corvette won at Talledega with Milt Minter behind the wheel and at the Daytona IMSA finale with Greenwood driving. Although reliability problems, mainly with the engine, plagued Greenwood's efforts during 1975, he nevertheless managed to win three SCCA Trans-Am races in a row and the Championship, proving again that when the car is right it is probably the world's fastest GT.

So the scene was set for the 1975 IMSA finale at Daytona International Speedway. Daytona has been the scene of some of Greenwood's most impressive wins and he was there to do battle against the likes of Peter Gregg, Al Holbert and Hurley Haywood in Porsche RSRs; Sam Posey, Brian Redman and Hans Stuck racing the indecently quick BMW CSLs and Al Unser and Allen Moffat driving the Horst Kwech-prepared Monzas. R&T was there also, not only to witness the final race in IMSA's most successful season to date, but for another in our series of production-versus-race-car comparison tests pitting Greenwood's ultimate plastic fantastic Corvette against a production 1976 Corvette.

For our track test Greenwood brought his new—virtually out of the box—1976 race car. Except for a brief shakedown on the skidpad and the banked 7½-mile oval of Ohio's Transportation Research Center (TRC), the car had never turned a wheel in combat.

The engine in Greenwood's IMSA car is an aluminum block ZL1 454-cu-in. V-8 with a 0.060-in. overbore that results in a displacement of 467 cu in. It's equipped with Carillo rods, a Chevrolet crank reworked by Moldex, a General Kinetics camshaft and a timing chain and roller rockers from Isky. Pistons, heads, valves and valve springs are Chevrolet. The oiling system is a dry-sump design incorporating a Weaver four-stage pump. A handmade radiator, shorter but wider and thicker than the production Corvette unit, is used because it can be placed vertically for improved cooling. The usual coolers are fitted to the engine, differential and transmission.

Sitting atop the engine is a unique fuel-injection system featuring a crossram magnesium manifold with a fuel cooler built into the bottom and Lucas injection components. Under development for three years, Greenwood attributes his engine's tremendous horsepower (700 bhp at 6800 rpm) and impressively smooth and flat torque curve (peak torque is 620 lb-ft at 4000 rpm) to this unit.

Backing up all that horsepower is a heavy-duty Muncie M22 Chevrolet 4-speed transmission. Affectionately called the Rock Crusher in racing circles, the Muncie gearbox is used as bought except that it's taken apart to check clearances and tolerances and then hand reassembled. The final drive ratio is 2.73:1 and combined with the 28-in.-tall rear tires gives the car a top speed of 221 mph at 7000 rpm.

The First Four Decades of Racing Success

Unlike many race car conversions, Greenwood doesn't start with a street car which is then torn down to the bare chassis. Rather he buys a production Corvette frame, gussets it for strength and crash protection and modifies it to accept the engine which is relocated approximately 1½ in. to the right and back almost 1 ft.

Modifications to the front suspension are surprisingly few. The front suspension including control arms and attachment points is purely production. According to Greenwood, the production Corvette front camber curve is very good and although the race car is considerably lower than production the only thing changed (besides the expected switch to teflon bushings) is the steering geometry to achieve zero bump steer. The rear suspension is an all-new independent design featuring unequal-length upper and lower A-arms and coil springs in place of the production Corvette's transverse leaf spring. The production rear suspension has two big drawbacks for racing, Greenwood says: it results in a tremendous amount of squat and toe change during acceleration and braking. With Greenwood's design, the swing-arm length is considerably longer which means he not only has the ability to adjust to zero toe change but also can dial in 50-75 percent anti-squat.

A high-speed banked track like Daytona obviously calls for a different chassis setup than the more usual road courses the IMSA cars run on. On a track such as Riverside or Laguna Seca the ideal setup is one where the car handles equally well

PHOTO BY CHUCK SCHMIDT

whether turning left or right. For Daytona a little extra weight is jacked into the left side of the car to improve the handling on the banking. But you can't adjust the car strictly for the banking as you can with a NASCAR stocker or you screw up the balance in the infield section.

The car likes to be stiff Greenwood says, and he uses spring rates that are about 25 percent stiffer than the Daytona suspension package that Chevrolet developed several years ago when Corvettes first started running the Daytona banking. Special Koni shocks with adjustable collars to facilitate ride height adjustment are fitted all around and an assortment of front and rear anti-roll bars allows final suspension tuning for various tracks. Braking a 2900-pound racing car from speeds in excess of 200 mph is not an easy task. The huge disc brakes Greenwood uses were originally designed by Hurst-Airheart to halt 3700-lb NASCAR stockers and are the only brakes Greenwood has found that are capable of holding down his Corvette. The rotors are drilled, not to improve cooling, but because Greenwood feels this aids brake response. Dual master cylinders—normal race-car practice—are incorporated into the system with a bal-

Front fiberglass can be removed and installed without disconnecting radiator as on previous car.

Rotors are drilled to improve braking response.

Race car's rear suspension has unequal-length A-arms.

SPECIFICATIONS COMPARISON
Production & Racing Corvettes

	Production	Racing
Price	$7605	$35,000
General:		
Weight, lb	3610 (curb)	2885 (race)
Weight distribution (with driver), front/rear, %	49/51	47/53
Track, front/rear, in.	58.7/59.5	59.5/64.2
Length, in.	185.2	187.0
Width, in.	69.0	82.0
Height, in.	48.0	47.0
Ground clearance, in.	4.4	3.0
Usable trunk space, cu ft	4.4	nil
Fuel capacity, U.S. gal.	17.0	32.0
Engine:		
Bore x stroke, mm	101.6 x 88.4	109.5 x 101.6
Displacement, cc/cu in.	5737/350	7654/467
Compression ratio	9.0:1	11.8:1
Bhp @ rpm, net	210 @ 5200	700 @ 6800
Torque @ rpm, lb-ft	255 @ 3600	620 @ 4000
Carburetion/fuel injection	one Rochester (4V)	Greenwood Crossram
Fuel requirement	unleaded, 91-oct	premium, 102-oct
Drivetrain:		
Gear ratios:		
4th	1.00	1.00
3rd	1.23	1.27
2nd	1.61	1.64
1st	2.43	2.20
Final drive ratio	3.55:1	2.73:1
Chassis:		
Brake system	11.75-in. vented discs front and rear, vacuum assisted	12.1-in. vented discs front and rear
Swept area sq in.	498	497
Wheels	cast alloy, 15 x 8	Sterling; 11 x 15 front, 17 x 15 rear
Tires	Firestone Steel Radial 500, GR70-15	Goodyear Blue Streak; 24.5 x 10-15 front, 28.0 x 17-15 rear
Front suspension	unequal-length A-arms, coil springs, tube shocks, anti-roll bar	unequal-length A-arms, coil springs, Koni adjustable tube shocks, anti-roll bar
Rear suspension	lower lateral arms, axle shafts as upper lateral arms, transverse leaf spring, tube shocks, anti-roll bar	unequal-length A-arms, coil springs, Koni adjustable tube shocks, anti-roll bar
Instrumentation:		
Instruments	160-mph speedo, 7000-rpm tach, 99,999 odo, 999.9 trip odo, oil press., coolant temp, ammeter, fuel level, clock	10,000-rpm tach, oil press., oil temp, coolant temp, rear-end temp, voltmeter, fuel press.
Warning lights	brake system, door ajar, headlights, seatbelts, hazard, high beam, directionals	oil press., voltmeter, fuel press.
Accommodation:		
Seating capacity, persons	2	1
Seat width, in.	2 x 18.0	14.0
Head room, in.	35.5	41.0
Calculated data:		
Lb/bhp (test weight)	19.0	4.7
Mph/1000 rpm (4th gear)	22.1	29.6
Engine revs/mi (60 mph)	2720	2030
Piston travel, ft/mi	1575	1355
Brake swept area, sq in./ton	250	305

ance bar that allows the front/rear brake bias to be varied. Sterling alloy wheels are fitted all around, 11 x 15 in. up front and huge 17 x 15 in. at the rear. The racing tires are Goodyear Blue Streaks, 24.5 x 10-15 in the front and 28.0 x 17-15 rear.

The swoopy body bares a passing resemblance to a production Corvette but it's considerably wider and all surfaces are contoured for maximum downforce and minimum drag. This latest car incorporates a new level spoiler that replaces the big duck tail used previously. From his testing at TRC Greenwood discovered that the new design generates sufficient downforce

PERFORMANCE COMPARISON
Production & Racing Corvettes

	Production	Racing
Acceleration:		
Time to distance, sec:		
0-1320 ft (¼ mi)	16.5	13.9
Speed at end of ¼ mi, mph	87.0	128.0
Time to speed, sec:		
0-30 mph	3.4	4.0
0-60 mph	8.1	6.2
0-100 mph	23.6	9.8
Fuel economy:		
mpg	14.0 (normal)	4.0 (race)
Handling:		
Speed on 100-ft radius, mph	33.5	64.8 (267-ft radius)
Lateral acceleration, g	0.748	1.200
Speed thru 700-ft slalom, mph	59.1	na
Brakes:		
Minimum stopping distances, ft		
From 60 mph	160	123
From 80 mph	262	220
Pedal effort for 0.5g stop, lb	30	45
Fade, % increase in pedal effort, 6 stops from 60 mph		
@ 0.5 g	33	nil
Interior Noise:		
Idle in neutral, dBA	62	112
Maximum 1st gear	84	na
Constant 70 mph	75	na
90 mph	81	na

(around 1000 lb at 200 mph) with a tremendous reduction in drag. With a race weight of 2885 lb the Corvette gives away a lot to the considerably lighter Porsches, BMWs and Monzas, but 700 bhp and that aerodynamic body more than even the odds.

Purposeful is an apt description of the gutted interior. It contains a single bucket seat, a roll cage, a fire extinguishing system and the usual assortment of gauges, switches and fuses.

For the street-car portion of the test Chevrolet provided a bright orange 1976 coupe equipped with most of the items an enthusiast would want: high-performance L82 350-cu.in. V-8, close ratio 4-speed, a high altitude (high performance is a dirty word at Chevrolet these days) 3.50:1 axle ratio, power-assisted steering and brakes, lightweight aluminum wheels and the stiffer gymkhana suspension package.

In the past few years the Corvette has been somewhat emasculated as a result of emission regulations. The thundering 454-cu.in. V-8 is history, a 4-speed manual transmission can't be ordered in California and even the famed small block V-8 is only a shadow of its former self as catalysts, lower compression, retarded timing and the like have taken their toll.

In its 1976 emission trim the L82 engine produces only 210 bhp at 5200 rpm and 255 lb-ft of torque at 3600 rpm. But it still has forged pistons and cranks, special rods and heads and a bottom end that will withstand a lot of high-rpm twisting. So take heart. Even if the street version isn't as fast as it once was, the pieces are available from Chevrolet or people like Greenwood to turn it into a real runner.

Obviously confident of the durability of his latest creation,

Greenwood street conversion is next best thing to real race car.

Greenwood agreed to allow R&T to test his car the Wednesday *before* the IMSA race. While he and his crew finished sorting out the ride heights and tuning the engine, we turned our attentions to the production Corvette. We last tested a Corvette in February 1974 and as we expected this latest example is slightly heavier and about 0.5 sec slower, accelerating from 0-60 mph in 8.1 sec and covering the quarter mile in 16.5 sec. But that's still pretty impressive performance these days. We followed these acceleration runs with tests of braking, handling and noise.

Then it was on to the race car. With the fire extinguisher bottle removed the Engineering Editor contorted himself into a semi-uncomfortable position on the floor on the passenger side of the car and surrounded himself with the usual road testing paraphernalia. Greenwood made a few short bursts to clean the plugs and then he was ready for the acceleration tests. In today's era of rolling starts and with gearing set up for a top speed of more than 200 mph, Greenwood's Corvette just isn't set up for standing starts. To save the clutch and to keep the engine from stalling Greenwood had to feather the throttle for about 3-4 sec until the revs built up. This general reluctance to get underway is reflected in the figures: the stock Corvette took only 3.4 sec to accelerate to 30 mph, the 700-bhp race car needed 4.0 sec to reach the same speed. But from that point on it was no contest. Once over its bucking and snorting the Greenwood car exploded forward with a deafening din from 60 mph to 100 mph in under 10 sec and to 150 mph in exactly 18.0 sec. (The EE said his ears rang for three days following this incredible display of power and yes, he'll have ear plugs next time.) The street car took 23.6 sec to reach the century mark and had run out of power at 132 mph. Considering the horsepower, the race car's quarter-mile time of 13.9 sec isn't all that impressive. But the figure that is indicative of its true potential is the quarter-mile speed: an incredible 128 mph. And Greenwood believes that with the proper gearing and smaller tires his car would be capable of turning the ¼ mile in less than 10 sec at speeds in excess of 160 mph!

Although a race car seldom has to brake to a complete stop except in emergency situations, the Greenwood car passed this test with flying colors. It stopped from 60 mph in 123 ft and from 80 mph in a mere 220 ft, about 40 ft better than the excellent-braking street car.

The lateral acceleration figure for the street Corvette is for a similar model we tested on our usual skidpad in southern California. That 0.748g number isn't particularly high but we average the times going clockwise and counterclockwise and the Corvette had a carburetion starvation problem turning right. For Greenwood's car the lateral acceleration is based on a 267-ft radius skidpad at TRC because the race car won't run without coughing and sputtering on a 100-ft radius circle.

We only have an idle noise reading for Greenwood's Corvette. Our sound meter as well as the EE's ears were adversely affected by that 112-dBA value and we had to recalibrate the meter on our return to Newport Beach, California.

With the straight line performance out of the way we got on with our timed laps around the 3.84-mi Daytona sports car track which includes more than two miles of high-speed banking. For the street car we increased the tire pressures to their recommended high-speed settings of 26 psi front and 36 psi rear. Then Greenwood went out and turned a few laps in the 2:38 area to familiarize himself with the handling characteristics of the stock Corvette. Satisfied the car was running properly he then cut a couple of fast laps finishing with a 2 min 36.2 sec, or an average speed of 88.6 mph.

For the race-car laps Greenwood preferred waiting until practice and qualifying for the IMSA race that weekend as a few minor problems had been uncovered by our acceleration tests and he wanted his crew to have time to correct them. Following an unhappy practice session on Friday Greenwood took only three laps during his qualifying session on Saturday. His second lap was the fastest turned all weekend and set a new record for Daytona: a time of 1:52.05 for an average speed of 123.4 mph. That time put Greenwood's Spirit of Sebring 1976 Corvette on the pole by almost 1.5 sec over the 2nd fastest qualifier, Al Unser in a Horst Kwech Monza. The race itself was a walkaway for Greenwood's red, white and blue Corvette as he averaged 116.78 mph for the 250 miles and a 39.36-sec margin of victory over the 2nd-place finisher, Brian Redman in a BMW. Quite a performance!

We knew the race car would be lots faster than the stock Corvette and now we knew exactly how much faster: 44.15 sec. But that 88.6-mph average for an absolutely stock street car is impressive and Greenwood who had never before driven a stock Corvette around any race course came in from his laps mighty impressed.

"The car is very neutral," Greenwood said. "On the power it understeers just a hair. If I went into a turn and the back end started moving around I'd get on the power and the rear would stick right in just like the race car does. So that's a good feature. I was real surprised with the brakes," Greenwood continued. "I didn't get on them super hard but I could get on them anywhere and I was always braking too early. On braking, there was a bit of trailing throttle oversteer if I went into a corner real deep and got on the brakes. The back end started to squat and move a little—but the tail didn't come around and it was very controllable. That's the advantage of the A-arm rear suspension on the race car. It eliminates the toe changes that induce trailing throttle oversteer."

"With the g forces generated on the banking—I was running about 130 mph up there—the car naturally felt a little undersprung. The car got a little light but not to the point where it started to wander."

Stiffer springs, larger diameter anti-roll bars and a big front spoiler would improve handling significantly on a high-speed track like Daytona, Greenwood feels.

Having had considerable experience with racing on street radials, we asked Greenwood how the Corvettes GR70-15 Firestones work on a race track.

"The radials roll over on the sidewalls a little. And that's the thing I liked about the T/As; they didn't squat down when you cornered them hard. But these tires stick pretty well and are very predictable; they don't break away suddenly and that's an important consideration for driving on the street."

It's obvious from Greenwood's comments that Chevrolet has built a good sports car. But as Greenwood's race car so aptly demonstrates, it's usually possible to improve even a good thing. If you want to go GT racing, Greenwood will be happy to build you a duplicate of his car for around $20,000, less engine. If you're only interested in improved street performance or a car that looks like Greenwood's race car that's okay too because Greenwood's company markets an assortment of Corvette bodies, engine parts and suspension components including the complete A-arm rear suspension. Corvette drivers, the line to Greenwood's shop forms at the right.

Typical race car fare: large readable gauges, easily accessible fuses, fire extinguisher bottle, primary and back-up ignition systems on right door. Also note reverse lockout for shifter.

Crossram fuel injection manifold dominates top of engine.

THE FIRST FOUR DECADES OF RACING SUCCESS

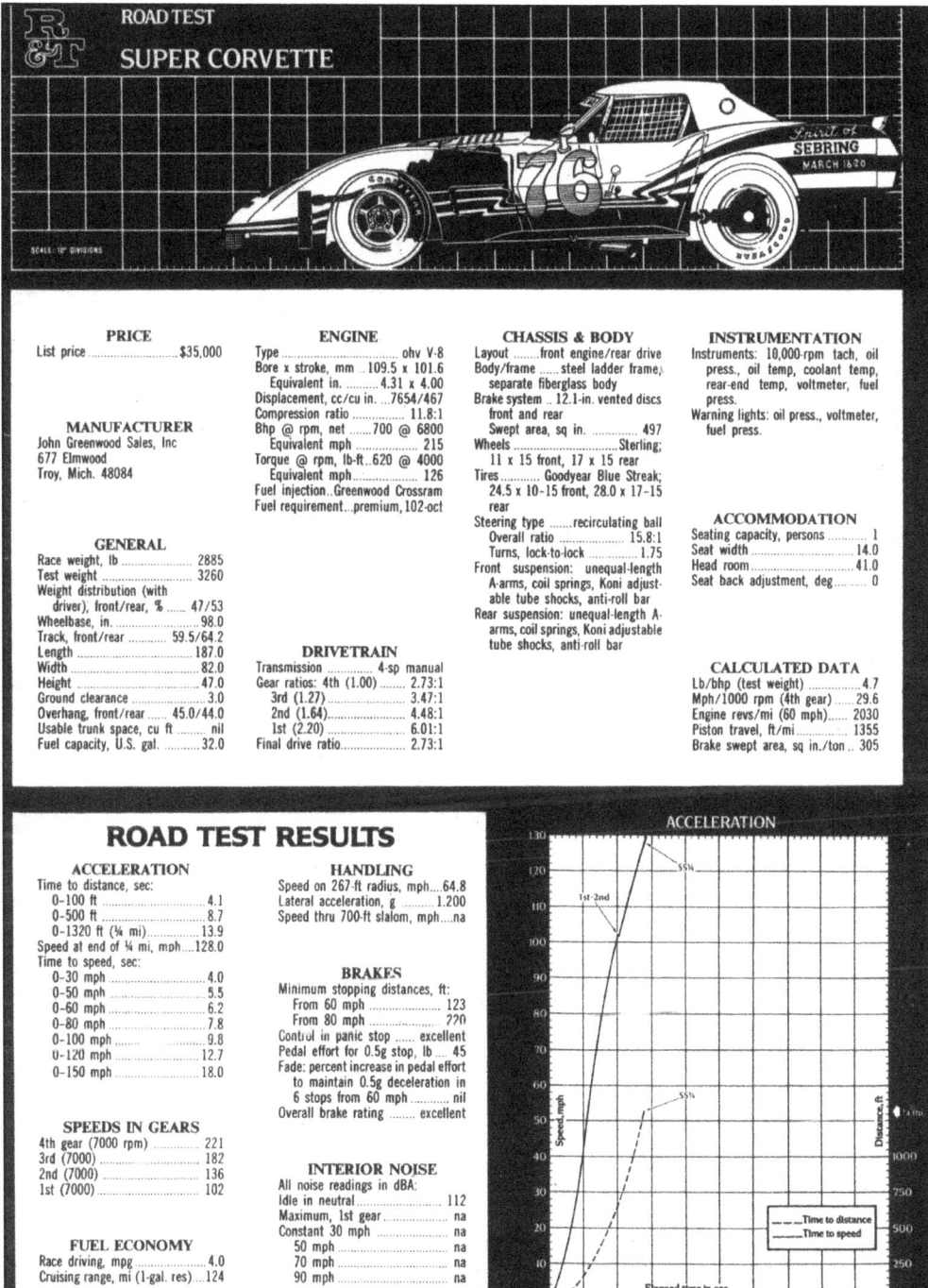

ROAD TEST
SUPER CORVETTE

PRICE
List price $35,000

MANUFACTURER
John Greenwood Sales, Inc
677 Elmwood
Troy, Mich. 48084

GENERAL
Race weight, lb 2885
Test weight 3260
Weight distribution (with driver), front/rear, % 47/53
Wheelbase, in. 98.0
Track, front/rear 59.5/64.2
Length 187.0
Width 82.0
Height 47.0
Ground clearance 3.0
Overhang, front/rear 45.0/44.0
Usable trunk space, cu ft ...... nil
Fuel capacity, U.S. gal. 32.0

ENGINE
Type .... ohv V-8
Bore x stroke, mm ..109.5 x 101.6
 Equivalent in. .... 4.31 x 4.00
Displacement, cc/cu in. ...7654/467
Compression ratio 11.8:1
Bhp @ rpm, net ...... 700 @ 6800
 Equivalent mph 215
Torque @ rpm, lb-ft..620 @ 4000
 Equivalent mph 126
Fuel injection..Greenwood Crossram
Fuel requirement...premium, 102-oct

DRIVETRAIN
Transmission .... 4-sp manual
Gear ratios: 4th (1.00) 2.73:1
 3rd (1.27) 3.47:1
 2nd (1.64) 4.48:1
 1st (2.20) 6.01:1
Final drive ratio 2.73:1

CHASSIS & BODY
Layout .... front engine/rear drive
Body/frame ...... steel ladder frame, separate fiberglass body
Brake system .. 12.1-in. vented discs front and rear
 Swept area, sq in. 497
Wheels .... Sterling;
 11 x 15 front, 17 x 15 rear
Tires .... Goodyear Blue Streak;
 24.5 x 10-15 front, 28.0 x 17-15 rear
Steering type ...... recirculating ball
 Overall ratio 15.8:1
 Turns, lock-to-lock 1.75
Front suspension: unequal-length A-arms, coil springs, Koni adjustable tube shocks, anti-roll bar
Rear suspension: unequal-length A-arms, coil springs, Koni adjustable tube shocks, anti-roll bar

INSTRUMENTATION
Instruments: 10,000-rpm tach, oil press., oil temp, coolant temp, rear-end temp, voltmeter, fuel press.
Warning lights: oil press., voltmeter, fuel press.

ACCOMMODATION
Seating capacity, persons 1
Seat width 14.0
Head room 41.0
Seat back adjustment, deg 0

CALCULATED DATA
Lb/bhp (test weight) 4.7
Mph/1000 rpm (4th gear) 29.6
Engine revs/mi (60 mph) 2030
Piston travel, ft/mi 1355
Brake swept area, sq in./ton 305

ROAD TEST RESULTS

ACCELERATION
Time to distance, sec:
 0-100 ft 4.1
 0-500 ft 8.7
 0-1320 ft (¼ mi) 13.9
Speed at end of ¼ mi, mph ...128.0
Time to speed, sec:
 0-30 mph 4.0
 0-50 mph 5.5
 0-60 mph 6.2
 0-80 mph 7.8
 0-100 mph 9.8
 0-120 mph 12.7
 0-150 mph 18.0

SPEEDS IN GEARS
4th gear (7000 rpm) 221
3rd (7000) 182
2nd (7000) 136
1st (7000) 102

FUEL ECONOMY
Race driving, mpg 4.0
Cruising range, mi (1-gal. res)...124

HANDLING
Speed on 267-ft radius, mph....64.8
Lateral acceleration, g 1.200
Speed thru 700-ft slalom, mph....na

BRAKES
Minimum stopping distances, ft:
 From 60 mph 123
 From 80 mph 220
Control in panic stop ...... excellent
Pedal effort for 0.5g stop, lb 45
Fade: percent increase in pedal effort to maintain 0.5g deceleration in 6 stops from 60 mph .... nil
Overall brake rating .... excellent

INTERIOR NOISE
All noise readings in dBA:
 Idle in neutral 112
 Maximum, 1st gear .... na
 Constant 30 mph .... na
 50 mph .... na
 70 mph .... na
 90 mph .... na

165

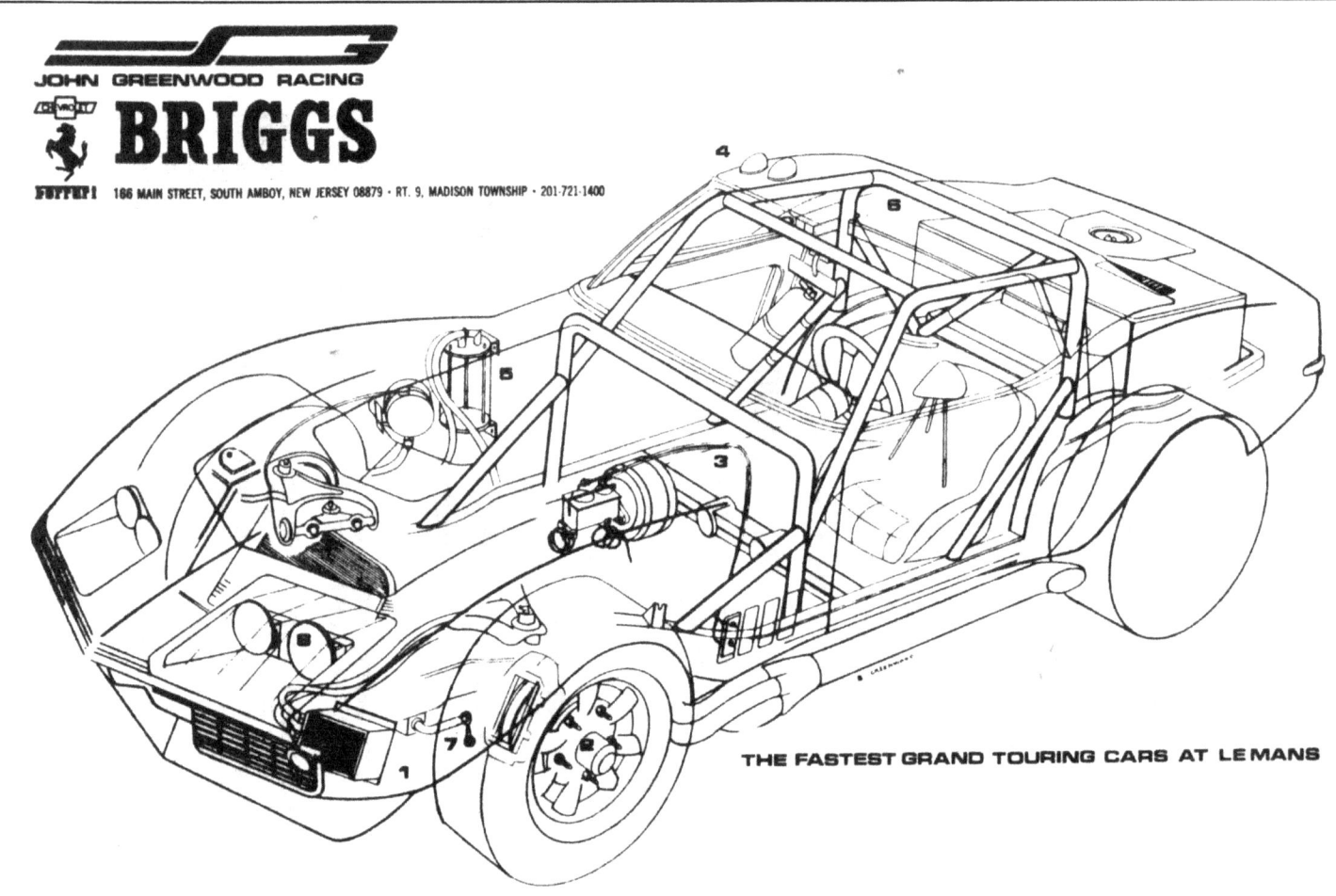

THE FASTEST GRAND TOURING CARS AT LE MANS

1. ENGINE OIL COOLER
2. WHEEL PILOT
3. VACUUM LINES FOR BRAKE PAD CHANGE
4. IDENTIFICATION LIGHTS
5. OIL CATCH CAN
6. ROLL CAGE
7. FRONT SWAY BAR
8. CIBIE LAMPS

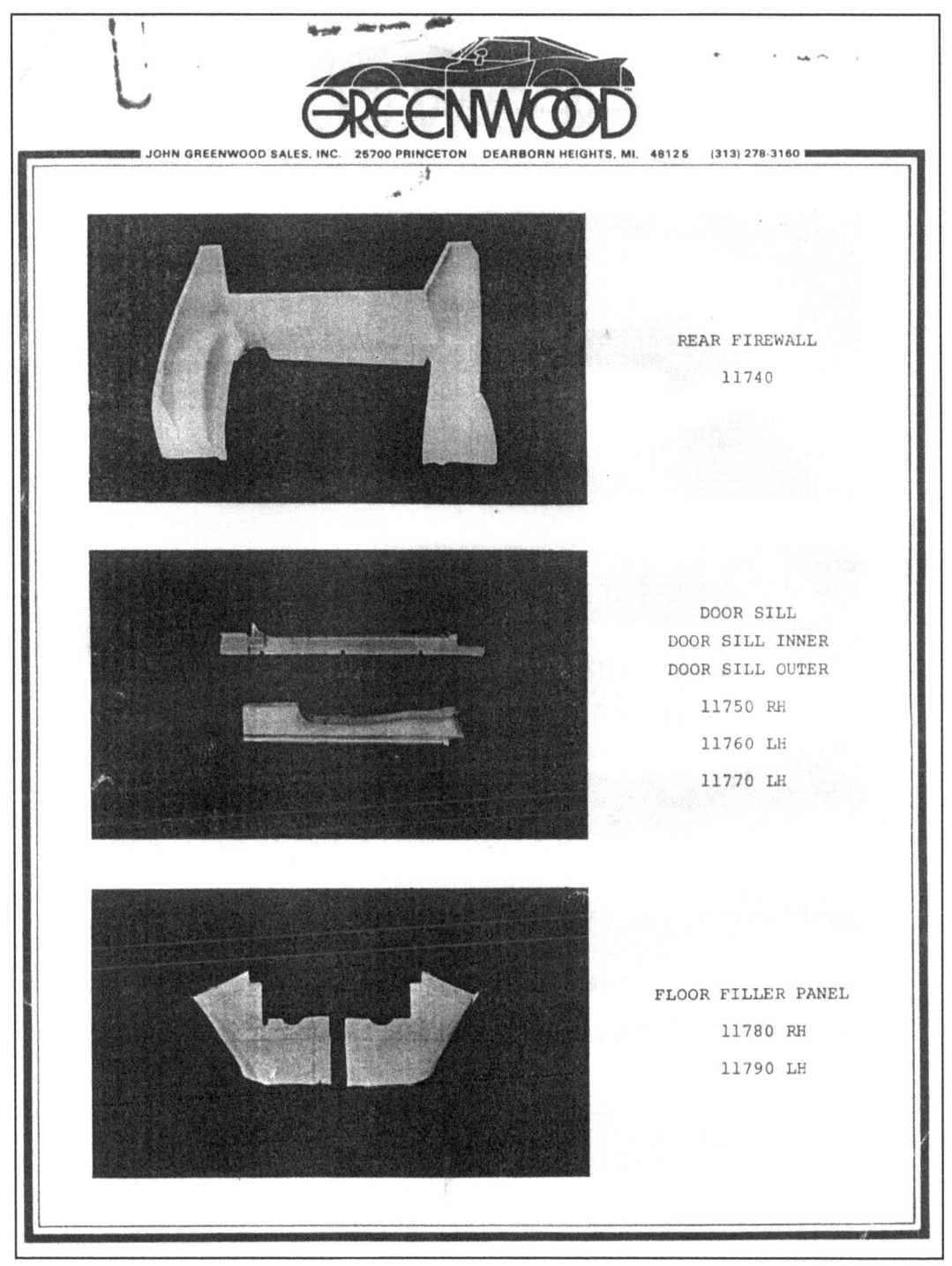

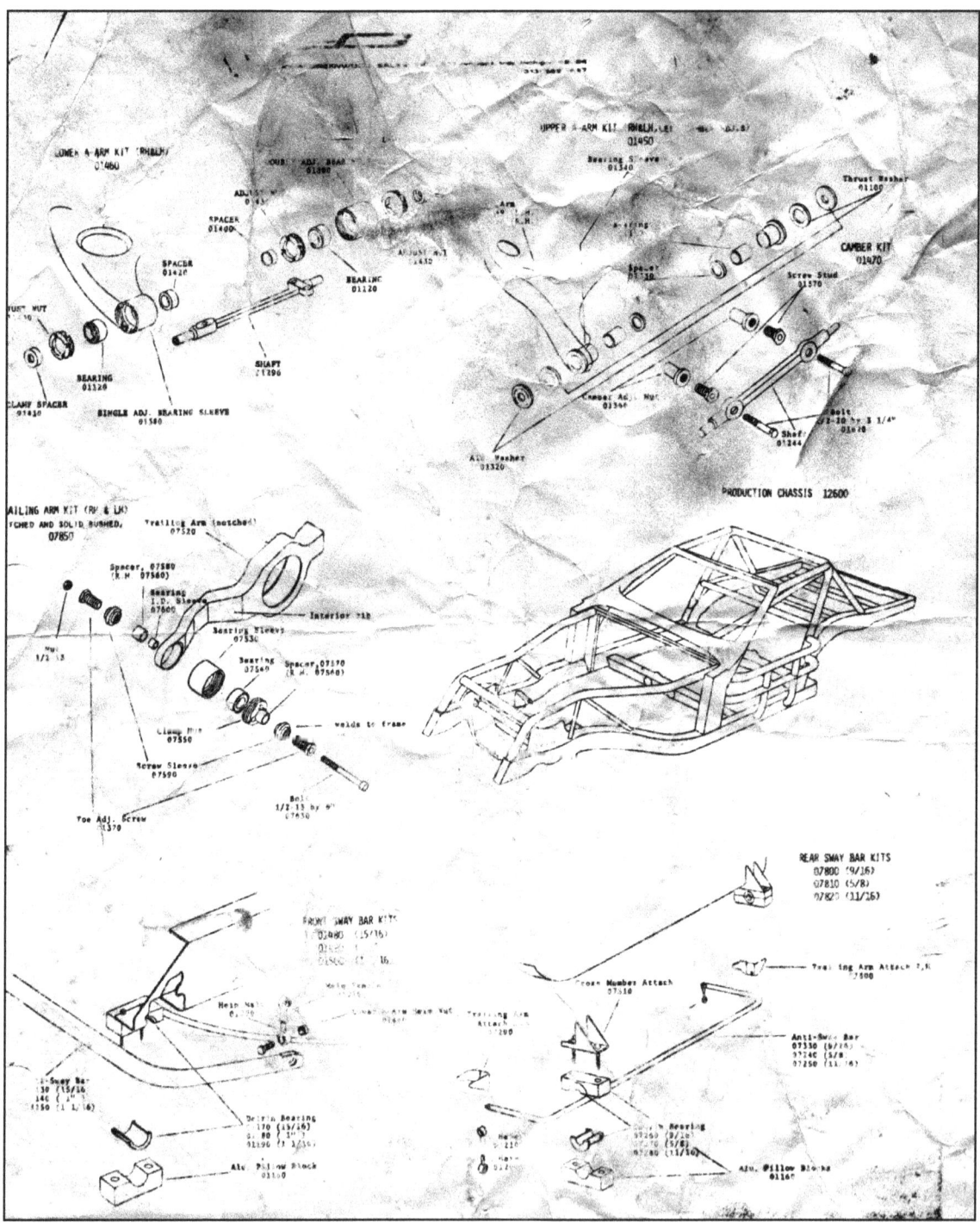

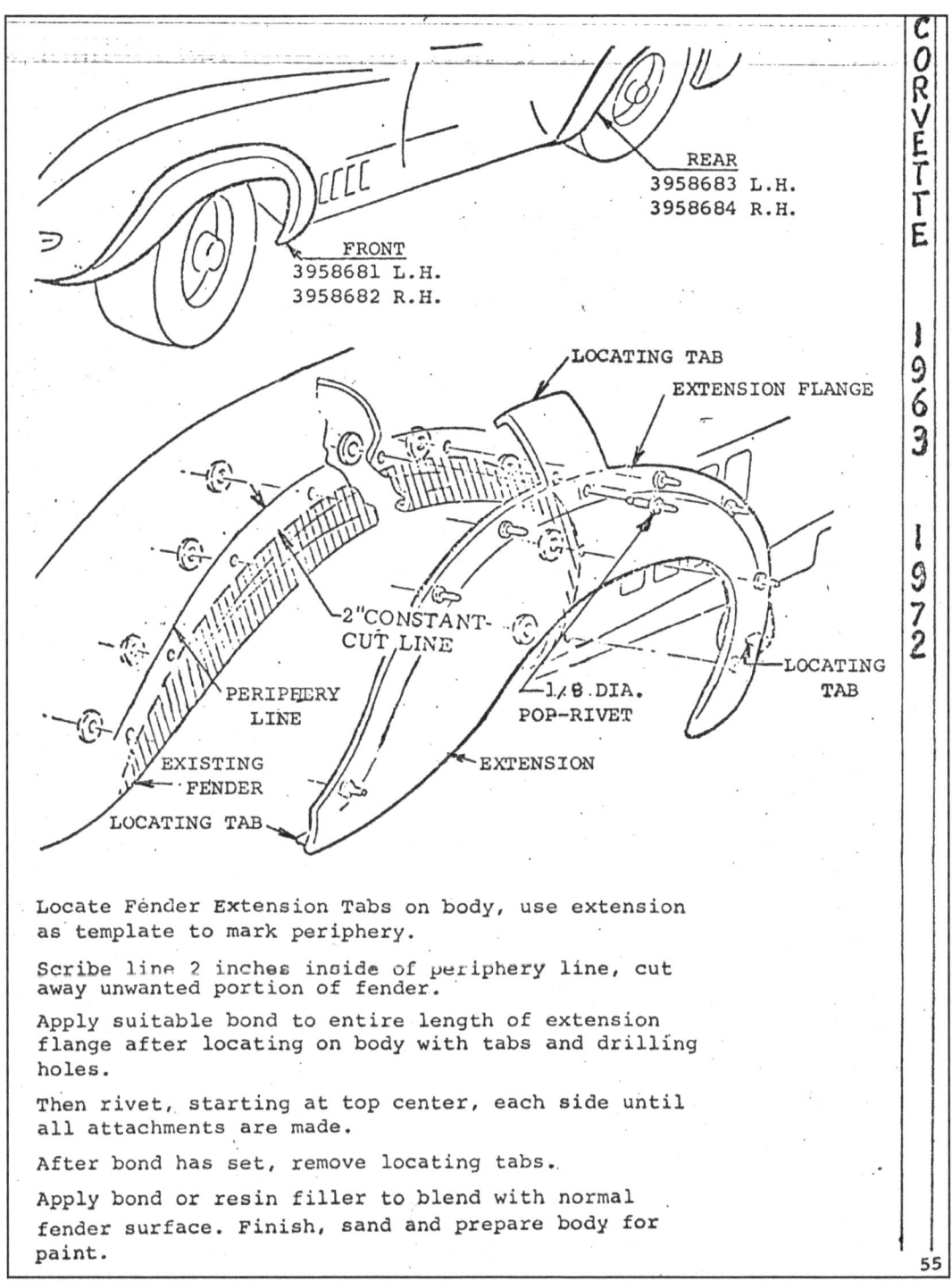

FRONT
3958681 L.H.
3958682 R.H.

REAR
3958683 L.H.
3958684 R.H.

Locate Fender Extension Tabs on body, use extension as template to mark periphery.

Scribe line 2 inches inside of periphery line, cut away unwanted portion of fender.

Apply suitable bond to entire length of extension flange after locating on body with tabs and drilling holes.

Then rivet, starting at top center, each side until all attachments are made.

After bond has set, remove locating tabs.

Apply bond or resin filler to blend with normal fender surface. Finish, sand and prepare body for paint.

JOHN GREENWOOD-BRIGGS
HI-PERFORMANCE PARTS*

After many years of extensive testing thru competition, JOHN GREENWOOD-BRIGGS now offer a complete line of parts and equipment for street use, drag racing and all types of road racing. Avoid the costly expense of mistakes and misconceptions in engineering and equipment application. Thru our experience, you have the advantage of buying the parts that have been proven successful on every level of competition time and time again. BUY THE BEST FIRST......JOHN GREENWOOD-BRIGGS HI-PERFORMANCE PARTS

Featured on the reverse side of this leaflet are some of the items included in our Corvette line - others are listed below.

ROLL CAGES

FIA, IMSA, SCCA APPROVED - COMPETITION TESTED AND PROVEN

- COMPLETE KITS
- ABBREVIATED ASSEMBLIES

SUSPENSION PARTS

- ANTI-SWAY BAR KITS - FRONT-REAR
- SHOCKS - DOUBLE ADJUSTABLE
- ALL SOLID, BEARING MOUNTED SUSPENSION COMPONENTS AVAILABLE

ENGINE-DRIVE TRAIN

EVERYTHING YOU NEED FOR COMPETITION OR STREET APPLICATION

- DRY AND WET SUMP SYSTEMS
- ENGINE OIL COOLER AND LINES
- TRANSMISSION OIL COOLER WITH PUMP AND LINES
- DIFFERENTIAL OIL COOLER WITH PUMP AND LINES

REPLACEMENT AND ACCESSORY ITEMS

- ALL FIBERGLASS BODY PARTS
- FRONT SPOILER WITH ALUMINUM AIR DUCTS AND HOSES
- STREET VERSION AVAILABLE

*For more information on the complete line of John Greenwood - Briggs Hi-Performance Parts just send $1.00 for a fully illustrated catalog and price list to:

John Greenwood-Briggs
166 Main Street
South Amboy, N.J. 08879
ATTN: Butch McKinnon

John Greenwood-Briggs
677 Elmwood
Troy, Mi. 48084
ATTN: Burt Greenwood

JOHN GREENWOOD SALES, INC.   25700 PRINCETON   DEARBORN HEIGHTS, MI. 48125   (313) 278-3160

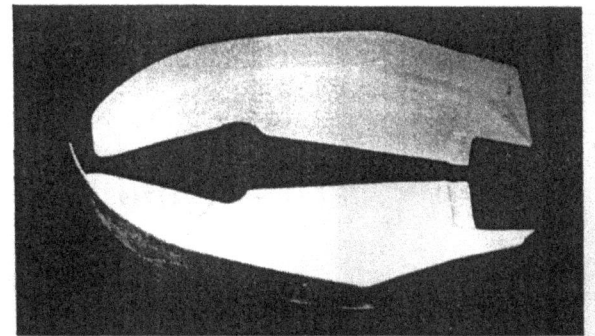

BULKHEAD SUPPORT
(LOWER)

11340 RH

11350 LH

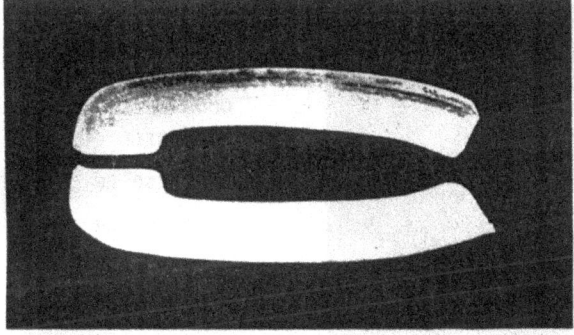

FRONT WHEEL WELL INNER
FENDER FILLER (FRONT)

11301 RH

11302 LH

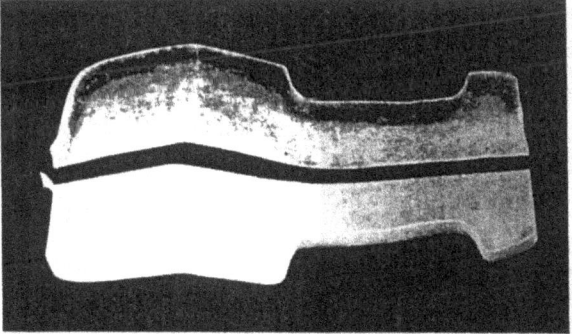

FRONT WHEEL WELL INNER
FENDER FILLER (REAR)

11303 RH

11304 LH

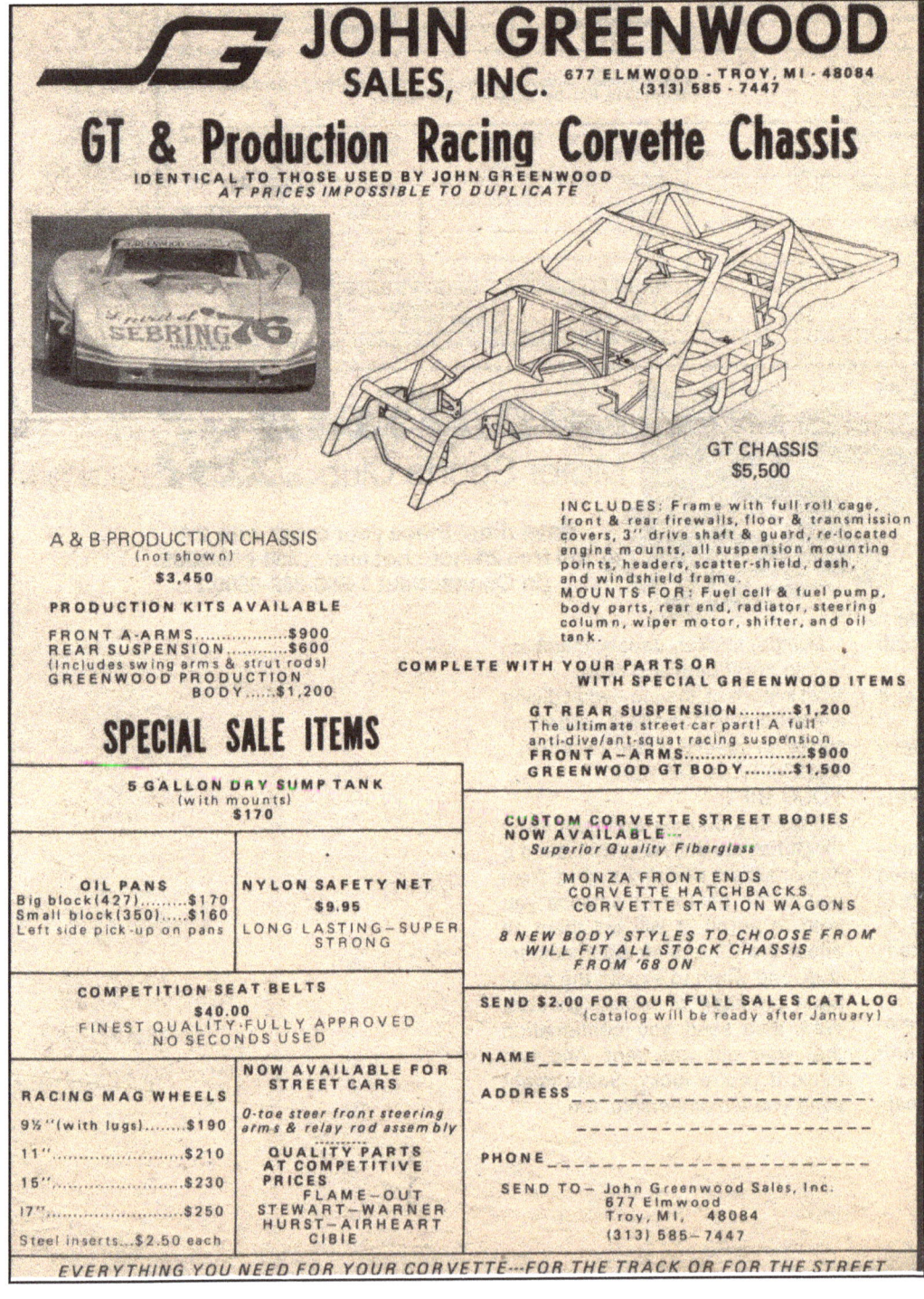

John Greenwood's shop during the early 1970s. [Photos: Courtesy of the Jack Boxstrom Collection.]

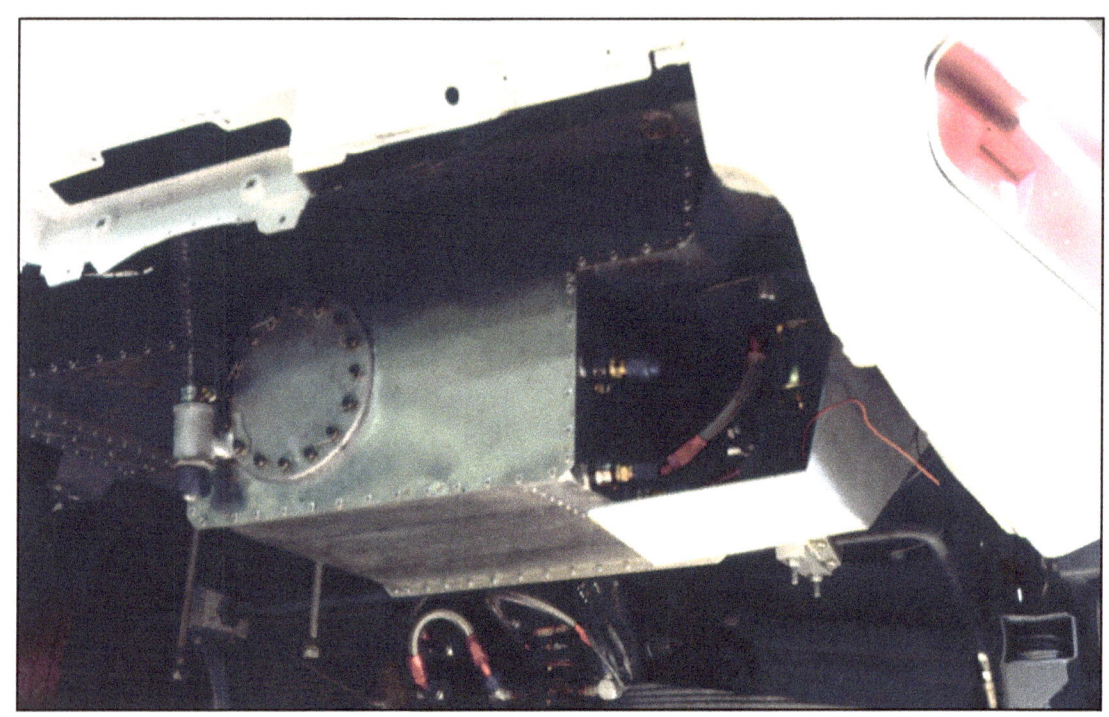

Above: A view from beneath the tail of a Greenwood Corvette, showing the complicated plumbing of the fuel tank.

Right: Fuel filler and breather on the trunk of the Greenwood Corvette.

[Photos: Courtesy of the Jack Boxstrom Collection.]

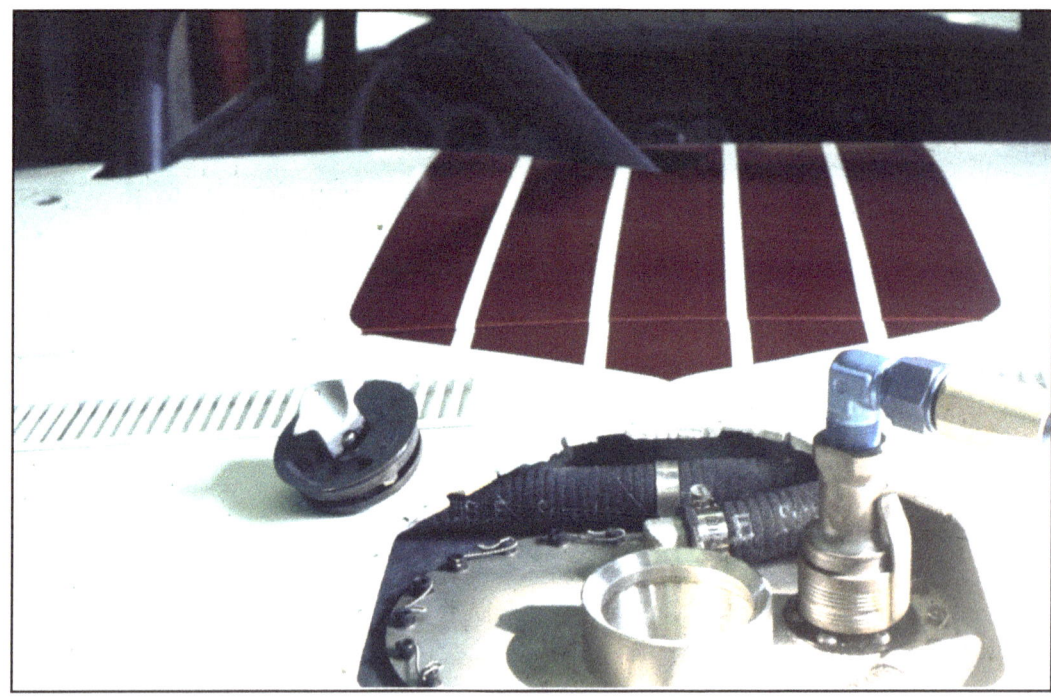

Appendix IV

Corvette Experimental Cars

There have been many Corvette show and experimental cars but as far as the racing versions are concerned, there are probably only two that could have been used on the track with success. The first one is shown above and is the Aerovette. This came very close to production and had the all-important mid-engine configuration. Sadly, when Duntov, Mitchell and Cole, retired in 1978 it was shelved, never to be used again.

Photographs are used courtesy of GM Media Archives.

Early styling sketches of what came to be known as the Corvette Indy. Designed in 1985, this brought together the Italian company Cecomp, Lotus and Chevrolet.

Zora Arkus-Duntov, standing alongside Dave McLelland (left), in front of the completed Corvette Indy. The car featured four wheel drive, four wheel steering, active suspension and ABS braking.

A styling sketch of the rear of the Corvette Indy.

The Corvette Indy under construction in Chevrolet's Research & Development Department. The construction was Kevlar/carbonfiber honeycomb for the monocoque, with electronic instruments and control systems.

The finished Corvette Indy. The engine was a twin-turbo V8, designed by Ilmor and giving approximately 600 horsepower.

The Corvette Indy. Such a shame it didn't make it into production.

www.ingramcontent.com/pod-product-compliance
Lightning Source LLC
Chambersburg PA
CBHW041410300426
44114CB00028B/2975